THE MUSIC OF THE NETHERLANDS ANTILLES

CARIBBEAN STUDIES SERIES

Anton L. Allahar and Shona N. Jackson

Series Editors

The Music of the Netherlands Antilles

Why Eleven Antilleans Knelt before Chopin's Heart

JAN BROKKEN

TRANSLATED BY SCOTT ROLLINS

University Press of Mississippi / Jackson

www.upress.state.ms.us

The University Press of Mississippi is a member
of the Association of American University Presses.

The publisher gratefully acknowledges the support
of the Dutch Foundation for Literature.

Nederlands
letterenfonds
dutch foundation
for literature

Originally published by Uitgeverij Atlas Contact,
Amsterdam

Manufactured in the United States of America

First English printing 2015
∞

Library of Congress Cataloging-in-Publication Data

Brokken, Jan, 1949– author.
[Waarom elf Antillianen knielden voor het hart van Chopin. English]
The music of the Netherland Antilles : why eleven Antilleans knelt
before Chopin's heart / Jan Brokken ; translated by Scott Rollins.
pages cm. — (Caribbean studies series)
Originally published: Waarom elf Antillianen knielden voor het hart
van Chopin / Jan Brokken. Amsterdam : Uitgeverij Atlas Contact,
?2005.
Includes bibliographical references and index.
ISBN 978-1-62846-185-5 (hardback) — ISBN 978-1-62846-186-2 (ebook)
1. Music—Netherlands Antilles—History and criticism. I. Rollins,
Scott, 1952– translator. II. Title.
ML207.N48B7613 2015
780.972986—dc23 2014017809

British Library Cataloging-in-Publication Data available

Chopin's death was not the end,
but just the beginning.
—Frederic Bastet

Solo: Brothers, let me sing
Chorus: Yes, give me a chance
Solo: Sing in our own rhythm
Chorus: Yes give me a chance
—Text from a Dutch Caribbean *tambú**

CONTENTS

TRANSLATOR'S NOTE

An explanatory note beforehand: In Dutch the word *Antillean* is commonly used to refer to the inhabitants of the former Dutch island possessions in the Caribbean—Curaçao, Aruba, Bonaire, St. Eustasius, Saba, and St. Martin. In a broader sense it can refer to someone from the Caribbean like it does in Spanish and French. The translator has opted to use Dutch Antillean to denote something specific to those islands.

✦ ✦ ✦

There is a glossary at the end of the book defining some terms unique to Curaçao and the Caribbean. Words found in the glossary are marked by asterisks (*).

THE MUSIC OF THE NETHERLANDS ANTILLES

1

A Polish Prelude

The news made it into the *Süddeutsche Zeitung*, even if it were only in the back pages, as a miscellaneous item above the featured articles. It was printed with a frame around it to draw the reader's attention to the bizarre nature of its content.

A Reuters correspondent had attended the mass held in the Church of the Holy Cross in Warsaw on the October 17, 1999, to commemorate the 150th anniversary of the death of Chopin. It had been a bitterly cold day and the invited guests, who filled the first seven rows, were not at all mournful about how briefly the service lasted: the church floor felt like a sheet of ice.

To be sure, Chopin is buried in Paris, at the Père-Lachaise cemetery, but in accordance with his last will and testament his heart was removed from his chest and brought back to Poland. The composer wanted to make it clear, once and for all and beyond his grave, that deep within he had always remained a Pole, even though he had left for Vienna and Paris as a nineteen-year-old, never to set foot again in his native land in protest of the Russian occupation. To make his exile complete, his body found its final resting place in French soil, under a handful of Polish earth that friends had given to him on the day of his departure from Warsaw. Chopin's mortal remains would never leave Père-Lachaise again, apart from that one hollow muscle, the most symbolic of all the organs.

Behind the sincere patriotic sentiments expressed in his last will and testament there lurked another reason, more gruesome to the point of morbidity. Chopin suffered from the fear of being buried alive, a phobia he had adopted from his father. In his thirty-ninth year, gravely ill and paralyzed with pain, he sensed that death was approaching. A few weeks before his passing he had requested Doctor Cruveilhier to perform an autopsy on his body immediately after being declared dead, and to cut the heart out of his chest. To remove any doubt whatsoever about an apparent death he also had put in his will that the lid to the casket could only be closed once his body had been embalmed. This measure took up so much time the composer could only be buried thirteen days after his death.

His carefully preserved heart—which, according to the doctor, was even worse off than his lungs that were ravaged by tuberculosis—was indeed brought to Warsaw and placed in the Church of the Holy Cross, enclosed in an urn which would survive the church's near total destruction almost a century later. In the final year of World War II bombs obliterated the chancel, nave, and a large part of the towers, but Chopin's heart remained unscathed.

After the reconstruction of the church, the urn was given a prominent place, in a niche near the altar. It was there the Bishop of Warsaw celebrated the mass on October 17, 1999. Besides his being every bit a Pole, Chopin had remained a fervent Catholic, receiving the proper sort of commemoration: with prayers, incense, liturgical hymns, and the sounds of the organ.

Another ceremony that honored the composer in equal measure was held a week after the mass, some fifty kilometers to the west of Warsaw at Zelazowa Wola, the country estate where Fryderyk Franciszek had been born. Six pianists took turns performing every one of Chopin's compositions for solo piano, in the house where his French father had given lessons to the children of Count Skarbek, and in the salon where Fryderyk had crawled across the floor, possibly even over to the piano. Candlelight recalled the atmosphere of those bygone days, and the listeners often found themselves looking outside, at the thick snowflakes falling on the paths and fields of the country estate, covering up the visible traces of this modern age, and at the farmhouse, diagonally behind the stately home, where Chopin's crib had stood. The Reuters correspondent had also covered this commemorative concert.

"Despite the bitter cold, some six hundred admirers of the composer attended the mass in the Church of the Holy Cross," he wrote. "After the sober ceremony some two hundred of those present undertook the pilgrimage to Zelazowa Wola, letting themselves be quietly transported in the company of Chopin's spirit to quiet reverie of three days of round-robin performances by six pianists of his polonaises, nocturnes, waltzes, mazurkas, scherzos, and ballads. Naturally there were quite a few Poles among those present, a few Germans and French, and the three inescapable Americans who never miss a commemoration, no matter whose it may be. Furthermore, eleven Antilleans knelt before the urn with the heart, in the Church of the Holy Cross, the majority of whom came down with severe colds in Zelawowa Wola, since they did not want to miss a single concert. No one from the organizing committee could explain the presence of this substantial delegation from the Caribbean."

I read the item in Munich, where it had been snowing just as heavily as in Poland, and felt the pangs of homesickness coming on. I still had to give a few more readings; then I packed my bags, returned to the Dutch Antilles and made the first notes for this book.

2

You Can Tell Just by Listening, Can't You?

Six years earlier, in July 1993, I had settled in Curaçao for an indefinite period of time, for no immediate reason, or maybe because of the melting pot of influences and cultures that make the islands in the southern Caribbean Sea seem so much larger than they really are. On those narrow strips of volcanic rock Europe, Africa, and South America merge, like solidified lava that owes its existence to various eruptions.

Curaçao lies so close to the South American coast that on certain days, usually after the rainy season, during the arid months of January, February, and March, you can see the mountains of Venezuela on the horizon, like a jagged edge above the water. You get the feeling of being able to touch the continent simply by leaning forward.

You notice the proximity of Latin America in everything, from the language spoken on the Leeward Islands and the flamboyant colors of the houses to the manners and mind-set. In contrast, the houses themselves, with their clock or step gables, the government buildings in neo-classical style, the brick offices built according to the principles of New Objectivity, the streets straight as arrows, the narrow alleyways and stately squares, all betray ties to Europe. Curaçao is multifaceted in a unique way: it unifies differences without removing them.

I spent my first three months there in a wooden house, in a village with the dreamy name of Lagun, at the foot of seven hills that form the coastline of the western part of the island, and at the mouth of a broad body of water with a mangrove swamp. It was as pretty as a picture postcard there and quiet, so quiet the only visits I got were on Sunday afternoons. For born and bred Curaçaoans I was living at the end of the world, or in any case too far from the capital city. Thirty kilometers separated me from the social and cultural heart of the island, which was only noticeably beating in downtown Willemstad. I realized that if I did not want to completely cut myself off, I had better move.

It was not all that hard to do. The house was in a deplorable state and I never succeeded in driving away the regular tenants—mice, rats, and iguanas. The corrugated iron roof leaked, the nylon-wool pile carpeting stank, the ceiling sagged and cracked under the weight of prehistoric reptiles. Even the peace and quiet was relative: I lay awake half the night wondering whether the crack junkie would roll the sliding door off its runners again, trying to scrape together a meal in my kitchen. Once he opened the wrong door and came into my bedroom. I must admit, he apologized profusely on the spot and took off faster than I could jump out of bed, though holding a knife in his hand, and from that point on I never felt completely safe.

I did, however, have to say farewell to an unencumbered view of the turquoise sea and four sheltered bays in the immediate vicinity. I could see the bay at Jerémi from my window, and every morning I was witness to a *brua* ritual. Under a *dividivi* tree bent by the wind that cast a long shadow across the beach, an elderly woman knelt, setting out her sacred stones and offering her sacrifice, usually a chicken whose throat had just been cut. She was seldom disturbed; a property developer had recently bought the land surrounding the bay and had closed off the entrance to the narrow beach with an iron fence. *Brua* literally means witchcraft; it is related to voodoo and practiced by the descendants of slaves. To me it felt like a piece of Africa had moved here with me, since before living in the Dutch Antilles I had seen animist priests offering the same sacrifices in the savannahs of Burkina Faso, Mali, Ivory Coast, and the jungles of Gabon. My move to the city cut me off from those rituals—*brua* was practiced only outside the villages or in the Hato caves—and in a certain sense brought me that much closer to Europe.

After looking for several weeks, I finally found a bungalow on the northern outskirts of Willemstad in a genuine middle-class Curaçaoan neighborhood. I got a one-year lease on a house in Kaya Tapakonchi from the sculptress Hortence Brouwn, who was just about to leave for Italy to buy marble and spend the entire winter, spring, and summer chipping away at it in Tuscany, in the direct vicinity of all the works of Michelangelo. Hortence had grown up in Suriname, which I could tell by a glance at framed photographs hanging on the walls of her hallway that held pictures of her black father and Javanese mother clad impeccably in white, standing in Paramaribo in front of their white house, a wooden building with a spacious porch. These photographs were from the colonial era—and I understood why they made Hortence feel homesick when she told me of her flight from the country. In 1981, her partner, a young lawyer, had made critical remarks about the military regime, and in 1982 he was one of the victims of the December murders.* Before the end of the year, Hortence fled to Curaçao, followed in exodus by several hundred fellow Surinamese in 1983 and 1984.

In her new surroundings Hortence became fascinated by the monumental breasts of Antillean women, perhaps because she herself so was slender. She duplicated the shapes in white, gray, and black stone. Her yard was full of them: breasts bereft of their pedestals. Immediately behind the statues stretched the *mondi,** full of man-sized, arid, prickly cacti, that only served to heighten the contrast. But I did not choose the house because of seductive torsos in a prickly décor, nor for the plaster statue on the porch of a woman with a matriarchal bosom and gigantic buttocks.

There was a piano in the living room, a tropic-proof Pleyel. No sooner had I moved into Hortence's bungalow than I slid behind the keys. It was just as hot late that evening as it had been halfway through the afternoon; the doors and shutters were all wide open, and the sounds of the piano must have been clearly audible at some distance. The bungalow had no windows.

The next morning the neighbor came to introduce himself. "It's great to have you as a neighbor," he said, "you are a real *yu di Kórsou.*"* A native child? A child of Curaçao? He noticed my astonishment and smiled at me as though I could not fool him. "I heard you playing last night and you were playing *our* music." Well now, I thought, this guy must have balls of cotton in his ears, because I had been indulging myself in a couple of mazurkas by Chopin.

I said nothing. I considered it a stroke of good fortune the neighbor had not complained about my playing so loud, or at having played at such a late hour.

And so I remained in ignorant bliss for weeks on end.

Like most newcomers I thought Curaçaoans only danced to salsa and merengue. Whenever I switched on the car radio all I heard were the imported hits from Venezuela, Colombia, and Santo Domingo, interspersed with the occasional Venezuelan bolero or Cuban son. The only thing that surprised me at first was the ease with which my neighbors could indicate what the various rhythms were.

Behind the hedge of cacti in the mondi, at a distance of about one and a half kilometers, were the huge festival grounds. Whenever a band was playing, my mattress trembled on waves of sound. On one occasion Kassav were playing, a group from Guadeloupe who played practically every number in the beat of their local rhythm known as *zouk*. The show lasted into the wee hours. "Had a great time dancing," said my neighbor the next morning. Just like me, she had been unable to fall asleep because of the constant thumping sound, but instead of tossing and turning in bed, Noris, a school teacher in her late forties, had got out of bed and let her feet pitter-patter across the cement floor of her porch.

"Do you know how to dance zouk?" I asked.

She clapped her hands, bellowing with delight: "*Ay Dios, no*; you can tell just by listening, can't you?!"

My neighbor—who lived in between Noris and me—could also tell just by listening that first evening. I had been playing a certain rhythm. I had played mazurkas. Music to dance to. Caribbean music.

3

The Faintest Idea

During the hottest part of the rainy season, in the last week of November 1993, I was sitting on a hard pew of the Fortkerk under a sky blue ceiling, not far from the chancel, one of four hundred in attendance. The audience—young, old, white, brown, black—were cooling themselves off with handkerchiefs and fans made of lace. The shutters were open; in the distance the bass whistle of a cruise ship resounded as it left the harbor, like a starting signal, or so it seemed, to the boisterous evening that lay ahead.

Cultural events are held on days of the week besides Sunday in that eighteenth-century Protestant church—in architectural terms a Dutch town church; in terms of color a white missionary's church in the tropics; and in its location inside Fort Amsterdam, directly opposite the government building, a fortified church built during the reign of the Dutch West India Company.

The events are organized by a committee, the key figure of which is Millicent Smeets-Muskus. Her snow-white skin is testimony to her Swedish origins in the village of Muskuse, near the border with Lapland; her family nevertheless has been living on Curaçao for over three centuries. Just like many descendants of those early colonists, the Muskussen have become confirmed patriots who cherish the local traditions as they would exotic plants.

That evening in November Millicent—or Dudi as she is called—had arranged a concert for six pianists from Curaçao, Aruba, and Bonaire. They had agreed among themselves that each would be responsible for playing works from a certain era. In two hours the entire history of Dutch Antillean classical music from 1850 to 1990 whirled past.

I heard waltzes, contradances, and mazurkas.

After the concert Dudi received guests at home. Once the pianists had quenched their thirst, they slid back behind the piano, one or even two or three at a time, improvising to their heart's content and turning the waltzes and mazurkas into a jam session. The atmosphere was lighthearted and exuberant; the older guests could no longer stay seated and began whirling through the room with youthful ease and timeless grace.

Among those making a night of it were August Willemsen, the Dutch translator of Fernando Pessoa, Drummond de Andrade, and Machado de Assis. He had come to Curaçao especially to attend a translation project. Papiamentu, the language of the Leeward Islands of the Dutch Antilles, resembles Portuguese and Spanish. Willemsen would be leading a number of workshops. I had met him on several occasions in Holland on the literary circuit there, or in the kitchen of a Brazilian girlfriend, who he helped prepare native dishes. Many years later our paths again would cross in Melbourne, Australia, where he had gone to begin a new life.

"What kind of colonizers are we?" Willemsen cried above the sounds of the piano. "How come we have never heard this music in Holland? The Portuguese know about Brazilian music, they are familiar with Villa-Lobos, but we haven't got the faintest idea that there is such a thing as an Antillean mazurka. These islands have belonged to Holland for over 350 years, much longer than Brazil was a part of Portugal. And we know nothing, we cannot believe our ears. I don't know about you but I am really starting to feel a strong sense of indignation. As if I have been kept in the dark on purpose."

Even though he had partaken liberally of the local libation, he was making perfect sense. When it came to matters of culture, the Netherlands in its long colonial past had only possessed one colony: Indonesia. The other territories had just been conquered lands, populated by people with the status of mules and the cultural refinement of parrots.

Johnny Kleinmoedig was the youngest pianist that evening, thirty-one years old at the time, born in 1962. In the Fortkerk, sitting in the front row, were his black father and white mother, a touching sight: the black father tapping his foot in time to the music, the white mother, ever so softly, humming the melody to herself. Edgar

Palm was the oldest pianist, a bald, jovial, chubby man with a pair of glasses he must have bought back in the 1950s that were perched crookedly on his nose. Born in 1905, now eighty-eight, he was still full of vigor, at least behind the piano. Padú del Caribe (b. 1920), Wim Statius Muller (b. 1930), Dominico Herrera (b. 1931), and Livio Hermans (b. 1935) formed the links between the oldest and youngest generation.

Regardless of their ages, the pianists all played with their souls. I saw it, I heard it: this was music that belonged to its performers like an effervescent tradewind; this was music they had grown up listening to from the cradle, like a language you pick up while playing with it and that later you no longer have to make a conscious effort to learn. They played music for their pleasure, at the concert, after the concert; they played half the night, till the crowd of listeners had thinned and the servants began cleaning up the glasses. Of all the guests, the pianists were the last to leave, together with August Willemsen and me, for we did not want to miss a single note of the festivities nor a drop of the local punch.

4

Geniuses of the Right Hand

Five of the six pianists were also composers, as I immediately discovered that evening in November, since they each played some of their own works. They merely turned out to be the pearls among the grab bag of brooches, earrings, chains, and glitzy watches. Between them Edgar Palm, Padú del Caribe, Dominico Herrera, and Wim Statius Muller have more than four hundred works to their name, joined now in the long line of tradition by Johnny Kleinmoedig, who on a murderously hot Christmas Eve in 1982 had composed his first waltz.

Since the latter half of the nineteenth century, the working method of Dutch Antillean composers has remained the same. Like their European predecessors, they first write out the entire composition, complete with dedication, notations for dynamics, time signature, and finger positioning. On the basis of the score, performers are then free to improvise. They first play what is written on paper, and then add their own inventions—just like Chopin and Liszt had done in their day and age.

There were stacks of sheet music on Hortence Brouwn's piano. I found quite a few Curaçaoan waltzes, dances, and mazurkas among them. I started studying several of them, inspired as I was by that scintillating concert in the Fortkerk. The pieces were not as easy as I thought. Possessed of a natural lilting quality, the melody sticks easily in the memory; at the same time they are melancholic in tone, and that mood perfectly matches languid tropical nights. But you need nimble fingers to be able to play them with panache.

While plodding away at the mazurka *Giselle* by Edgar Palm and at one of the countless runs in the intensely wistful waltz *Despedida* (Departure) by Wim Statius Muller, I was reminded of a statement by the pianist Arthur Schnabel, which was often cited with pleasure and approbation by Glenn Gould: "Chopin, the genius of the right hand . . ." To Schnabel and Gould, Chopin's left hand merely prances along, while the scores by Bach, Beethoven, and Brahms are blueprints for cathedrals, of monumental constructions buttressed equally by both hands.

Dutch Antillean composers followed Chopin's example. When I started studying the pieces, I understood why: they never forgot that the left hand must always keep the dance rhythm. Without that prancing left hand the character of the music would be lost.

A few months later I heard Wim Statius Muller again, at someone's home. In the meantime I had grown used to the custom of a pianist sitting down to play a series of requests for waltzes and various dances during receptions, celebratory occasions, or ordinary birthday parties. It could be Statius Muller, Kleinmoedig, Livio Hermans, Robert Rojer, or any amateur pianist. For lack of being able to find anyone better I was occasionally called upon to play; and even though I was fresh from Europe and not in the same league as the islanders, I overcame my timidity with the thought that a Curaçaoan would rather hear an imperfect rendition of *Despedida* than nothing at all.

Statius Muller played one of his own mazurkas and this time I paid more attention to the rhythm he followed.

A memorable quarrel had taken place in Paris in 1842. Chopin was giving a lesson to a student in the house of the composer Giacomo Meyerbeer when the latter suddenly burst into the room. The student, Wilhelm von Lenz, had been practicing the mazurka opus 33 no. 3; Meyerbeer sat down and Chopin asked Von Lenz to begin again. "He is playing in two-four time," said Meyerbeer, "and it's a mazurka, so he should be playing in three-four time." Chopin became angry and asked Von Lenz to start over again, this time keeping time furiously with a pencil in his hand. A purple blush spread over his pale cheeks. As a rule, Chopin never lost his temper; he was the embodiment of amiability itself and always whispered to his students, when all of a sudden he started shouting like some querulous person indulging in his pet peeve: "It's in three-four time; it's in three-four time." His eyes blazed with anger. Meyerbeer watched the storm pass with the look of satisfaction on the face of someone who knows he is right. Indeed, Chopin had the tendency of slipping into two-four time when playing mazurkas, even though they are clearly written in three-four. That was because he often held the second beat quite a bit longer. He made the mazurkas sound more rhythmic than they were on paper.

Statius Muller did exactly the same.

5

A Port of Transit

Caribbean island music had that which I have always sought in my travel writing: it clearly expressed how cultures shade into one another.

At the end of the eighteenth century, European frigates setting sail for the Caribbean islands brought all sorts of musical forms with them that had already crossed several borders on the old continent. For example, the English *country dance* had spread out across all of Western Europe, and on the other side of the Channel, owing to a faulty translation, was erroneously called *contradanse*. The French contradanse sailed to Saint-Domingue, which had become a wealthy colony because of sugar cane, and underwent African-influenced transformations in the plantation houses. The monotonous rhythmic thump was syncopated and changed into a rolling beat.

A great deal of music was made on the Caribbean islands. It was the only form of entertainment, certainly on the remote plantation houses. Practically every country estate had a spinet, later on a piano, and not just for young ladies but young fellows as well. Whenever the planters went to the cities, they hurried to the stores where the latest sheet music was on sale. They were less interested in the gazettes, as they only contained old news; music was the slender thread that bound them to their country of origin: contradanses or minuets, printed in faraway Paris, but suddenly so close they could be performed in the homes of the urban citizenry or the backyards of the sugar farmsteads.

In accordance with the basic principles of the French Revolution, the Jacobins abolished slavery in the French colonies in 1793. They applied the principles of liberty, fraternity, and equality to all citizens of the French territories, regardless of the color of their skin or status. In several colonies the whites refused to obey this decree, and in the end Napoleon would rescind the measure at the insistence of his beloved Joséphine de Beauharnais, who in turn was under pressure from her relatives in Martinique. The whites of Saint-Domingue had long since sought the help of the English, not only France's archenemy, but the insatiable great power that lay claim to every single island in the West Indies. The slaves revolted against the English occupation in Saint-Domingue, led by Toussaint L'Ouverture. He declared it the first black republic and changed its name to Haiti. Most whites died in the fighting, were slaughtered, or fled to Martinique, Guadeloupe, New Orleans, Curaçao, Trinidad, and especially to Oriente, the easternmost province of the Spanish colony of Cuba. It was there the *contradanse* intermingled with the songs of love and death from the Iberian peninsula.

In Oriente the *contradanza* had much more of a lilt than the original contradanse. It was more passionate, more whimsical—though not totally. The first section remained as it had been originally—bare, cool, restrained; passions were not unleashed until the second section. The first section remained Western European, the second became Cuban. When listening to a *danza* you can actually hear the journey the music has made.

The journey did not stop in Oriente. From Cuba the *danza* spread out over the entire Caribbean archipelago and large areas of South America, via Curaçao, which fulfilled the role of a port of transit. Practically every cargo and mail vessel bound for La Guaira, Belém, Recife, Montevideo, Buenos Aires, or Valparaiso called in at the island. Cargo and parcel post from other islands were loaded in the port of Willemstad, the largest in the Dutch Antilles. It was just as easy to take onboard the sheet music hot off the local presses, or the Spanish-language weekly *Notas y Letras*, also published on Curaçao.

The island may have been part of the Kingdom of the Netherlands, but the number of inhabitants originally from the mother country could be counted on the fingers of a couple of hands. Not until Shell Oil set up its refinery in 1918 did a Dutch district arise, called Emmastad, and thirty years later a second one, Julianadorp; before that, colonial authorities and military garrison lived together in Fort Amsterdam. Outside that enclave, most whites were Jewish or descended from Protestant colonists who had settled on the island between 1650 and 1750. The Jews married among themselves, as did those Protestants from the upper echelons of society. Lower-class Protestants were content with Venezuelan or "colored" partners. By the nineteenth century, however, the caste system was no longer viable owing to a lack of marriageable daughters. The whites with double surnames (the upper class) also opted for partners from the nearby continent. The Protestants became Latinized. Instead of staying at home over a cup of coffee discussing the sermon, their dances were now held after church services, and these weekly recurring parties went on from 11 A.M. until late into the afternoon. "No pen could describe the furious dances they engage in here. Old, young, everyone jumps in," the amazed Dutch lieutenant Van der Goes wrote home in 1830.

Among themselves the islanders spoke either Papiamentu or Spanish. Dutch was seldom heard in the streets. Curaçao was home to a host of Spanish-language publications with such titles as *Noticiero, El Imparcial, El Comercio, El Liberal, La Ilustración, El Evangélico, Liberal, El Correo de las Antillas,* and—characteristic of its readers—*La Política Venezolana* or *El Eco de Venezuela.*

Notas y Letras was the most international. It had subscribers throughout Latin America. Unlike in Cuba, ruled with an iron fist by Spain, there was no longer censorship in the Dutch colony. The Cuban governor general held his own with the South American dictators, nipping all resistance in the bud and only giving permission for a performance of Bellini's opera *I Puritani* when the word *libertá* had been substituted by the female name *Lealtá.*

Because of the total freedom of the press on Curaçao, *Notas y Letras* could become the tribune for South American liberals. Besides its irreverent words, it also came with notes: musical scores were printed in the mid-section of the magazine. Countless Caribbean composers published their dances, waltzes, and mazurkas in *Notas y Letras.*

No Argentinean wants to believe it, but initially the tango was much more popular in Willemstad than it was in Buenos Aires. In the second section of his *danza,* the Curaçaoan composer Jules Blasini often made use of the tango rhythm. Long before Argentineans let their hair down with the tango, Blasini had Curaçaoans dancing to this rhythm. He published his works in *Notas y Letras*—undoubtedly to the utter amazement of its Argentinean readers: in

Buenos Aires the tango was only danced in clandestine locations and only by men.

Notas y Letras' libertarian ideals did not get in the way of the commercial basis underpinning the weekly publications. The publishers, the four sons of Agustín Bethencourt, were keen to have as many copies as they could roll off the presses their father had founded. Father Bethencourt had fled from Venezuela for political reasons; in Willemstad he carried on the liberal offensive he had initiated on the mainland.

Curaçao had enjoyed a liberal reputation ever since 1812, when Simón Bolivar went into exile in Willemstad. During their three-month stay at the sparsely furnished house at Motetberg, he and his four fellow refugees were free to plan the liberation of South America, beginning with a series of battles in 1813 and ending in 1824 when the Spaniards departed. Bolivar's two sisters stayed on Curaçao much longer, living on Curaçao until 1819 in an eight-sided house known as the Octagon.

A procession of exiles followed El Libertador's example. In 1821, two thousand monarchist Spaniards settled on Curaçao. They transformed the Otrobanda district into one huge casino, moving on two years later, tired and broke from rolling the dice, to Cuba, Puerto Rico, or Spain. The founders of the Dominican Republic, Juan Pablo Duarte, Juan Isidro Pérez, and Pedro Alejandrino Pina, lived on Curaçao before starting the revolution in 1844. Yet another civil war broke out in Venezuela, this time in 1845, and seven liberal politicians sought refuge on Curaçao. In 1858 the federalists fled to the neighboring island, including the future president of Venezuela, Antonio Guzmán Blanco. He moved into a building behind the post office in Otrobanda and gave refuge to so many freedom fighters there that the Venezuelan government threatened to invade Curaçao. Requests to have him extradited were refused, however, and Guzmán Blanco was finally able to return to Caracas as a free man. The black president of Haiti, who in 1852 had had himself crowned Emperor Faustus I, was forced to flee the country in 1865. He stowed away on the Curaçaoan schooner *Rigoletta* bound for Willemstad. Until his death he lived in the Keizershof (Emperor's Courtyard), a practically windowless complex he had had built above the Santa Annabai and Otrobanda. At an angle below that Dracula castle, the next generation of exiles settled in houses built in the style of Havana, with flat roofs that served as verandas. For those Cubans who were at odds with the colonial authorities, Curaçao was the preferred place of exile, for they could make themselves understood in their own language and enjoy a staggering array of Spanish-language periodicals and radical documents.

Curaçao emulated Amsterdam, which had given refuge to exiles and scarcely prohibited them from expressing their opinions, whether or not they were in writing.

The liberalization of South America was far from being achieved by the middle of the nineteenth century. The political climate remained gruesome, owing to dictatorships, coups d'etat, and civil wars. *Notas y Letras* advocated that South America proceed along the lines set down by Simón Bolívar and Francisco de Miranda. The revolutionary general De Miranda, who died in a Spanish dungeon in 1816, had been an excellent flautist who practiced his passion for music every evening, even on the eve of the battle he would lose through an act of treachery. To him, the struggle for freedom should also lead to the cultural revival of South America, an idea that Augustin Bethencourt also adopted.

Shortly after his arrival on Curaçao, Bethencourt set up a bookstore, a store selling musical instruments, a music and magazine publishing company, and a printing office. He owned a special typesetting machine that made it possible to print musical scores. It was his idea to establish *Notas y Letras*. He did not live to see the first issue, but his four sons took over the printing business and produced the weekly publication with its mid-section of musical scores, an absolutely unique publication in the huge area where it was distributed: from Santo Domingo to deep in the interior of Venezuela, from Puerto Rico to Argentina, Chile, and Peru.

Latin America was floating on a cloud of prosperity. The small army of generals and potentates had not yet ransacked its riches; it exceeded North America and other continents in terms of affluence. It exported coffee, cacao, sugar, meat, wood, bananas, gold, precious metals, and (toward the end of the nineteenth century) rubber. The standard of living of the middle classes was one and a half to twice the size of Western Europe; there was an opera house in practically every city, and nearly every merchant's home had a piano or even grand piano. The well-to-do, usually of Spanish descent, wanted to be entertained by infectious dance music. *Notas y Letras* supplied this demand, providing scores by Cuban, Puerto Rican, Dominican, Venezuelan, and Curaçaoan composers.

This weekly publication was of enormous importance to the development of Curaçaoan music. Not only could composers publish their work, but they could also count on having a wide audience throughout Latin America. Among the fourteen people that made up its staff were the pioneers of Curaçaoan music, the composers Jan Gerard Palm, Chris Ulder, and Jules Blasini. Joseph Sickman Corsen was the editor-in-chief, a poet-musician who went down in history as having written the first poem in Papiamentu. *Notas y Letras* did indeed spark a cultural revival.

The dances Corsen, Jan Gerard Palm, Ulder, and Blasini published in *Notas y Letras* were all influenced by Cuban music. In the first section, the *chaîne,* they remained Western European in terms of rhythm, somewhat sedate. Next came the transition to the melodious Iberian song theme in the second section. But—and this is the Dutch Antillean influence—in the third section they became much more rhythmic than the dances from Oriente; they were more hybrid, heterogeneous.

Curaçao intensified the African elements of the danza. In the second and third sections after the seventh chord comes the *cinquillo* rhythm, in two-four time with alternating triplets and two eighth notes. In the second section the cinquillo is still played in a somewhat restrained manner, but in the third section the rhythm cuts loose. The beat alternates from 5/8 to 6/8 and becomes just as ambivalent as in the *tambú,* the drum music to which the African slaves on Curaçao danced.

The waltz, too, was also rendered with more fiery rhythm, and not always in 3/4 but often in 6/8 time. That had to do with the temperament of the dancers, but also was due to the available space. The dance salons in the Caribbean country estates were quite small compared to European ballrooms; because they were smaller, steps had to be made more quickly. This explains the 6/8 beat.

6

As Melancholic as a Sunset

One European composer was an instant hit when his work reached Oriente, Havana, Saint-Pierre, San Juan, and Willemstad. The primary reason was that he was able to elevate all sorts of banal dances into sublime forms of music.

Chopin was best suited to the Caribbean temperament, with his mix of volcanic fire and cooling wistfulness, of refinement and rhythm, of melody and dance. To a Caribbean islander, music is only music if you can dance to it, as is certainly the case with waltzes and mazurkas. Consequently, Caribbean composers started composing waltzes and mazurkas in great numbers.

Polish dances were used by European composers from Rameau to Mozart, long before Chopin was born. They even enchanted Johann Sebastian Bach, who composed a polonaise in his Leipzig period. Chopin heard the simple harmonies at their source: the peasant weddings and harvest feasts he attended on the country estates of his friends in the region around Warsaw. The polonaise and mazurka were excellent vehicles for him to use in his attempts to radically implement musical innovations without shedding traditional structures. Within the fixed confines of a dance form they offered him great stylistic freedom, and he was able to ingeniously exploit them to the fullest.

The mazurkas became, as Benita Eisler wrote, "the laboratory of the alchemist." They were a place where Chopin could experiment with expanding the traditional structure of the dance form, but where he could also play with fire. He kept erupting out of strict rhythmic confines, leaning more toward the volatile, the asymmetrical, to mutant forms and sharp dissonances, allowing them to accelerate at a feverish pitch before collapsing in the end. In the words of Benita Eisler, his mazurkas "complied with the ultimate demands of the romantic: 'beauty that is touched by the exotic.'"

Chopin already had something in him of the jazz musician who thrives on balancing at the cutting edge of every single measure. His contemporaries had a hard time accepting that aspect of his playing. Even Hector Berlioz, himself an innovator and upstart in many ways, complained in his autobiography like an old schoolmaster about some young whippersnapper: "If you ask me, Chopin has pushed rhythmic freedom far too far."

Chopin was just as quirkily adept at turning his hand to waltzes. During his stay in Vienna, he witnessed the rise of Johann Strauss Sr. and in a letter to his father he wrote: "They call a waltz a 'work' here." He thought the Viennese waltz constituted bad taste, but he could not resist exploiting the stuffy one-two-three beat with as many melodic options as he could. In the final analysis, the polonaise was also rhythmically boring. Chopin had already begun experimenting with it at the age of eight and did not rest until he had composed his *Grande Polonaise Brillante*, a brilliant piece indeed, and just as impetuous as his *Grande Valse Brillante*.

The fact that he stuck so stubbornly to the dance beat, while at the same time treating it with such freedom, is what made him appeal to Caribbean composers. But they also recognized other facets of themselves in him: the Pole who had fled to France and ended up in between two worlds. He may have been the son of a Frenchman, but he had not spoken much French in his childhood. His father was just as patriotic as a born and bred Pole; he owed his upbringing and his career to a Polish family and considered himself one of them. Without the care of the Weydlich family, Nicolas Chopin would have taken over his father's vineyard and remained just as illiterate as all the other small winegrowers of the Lorraine.

Owing to the cunning machinations of politics involving marriages between European royal families, the duchy of Lorraine was bequeathed to the former king of Poland in the second half of the eighteenth century. A Polish count took up residence in a castle near the village of Marainville; his secretary Weydlich took a shine to the young Nicolas, saw to his education, and took him with him to

Poland in 1787. Nicolas was sixteen and left to avoid military conscription. In Warsaw he extended his knowledge of French and Polish literature, became adept at mathematics and music (he was an excellent flautist), and took part in the first Polish popular uprising in 1794. The noble, upper-class families saw in him the perfect home tutor: French by birth, Polish by disposition. He took up a post with Count Skarbek and moved to Zelazowa Wola, married a Polish domestic servant girl, and became father to a son and three daughters, to whom he all gave Polish names. He taught the Skarbek children French, and spoke Polish at home. In Warsaw, too, where he had found a better position, he refused to speak a word of French, even though it was the *lingua franca* of the upper echelons of society. The fear of being mistaken for a foreigner hounded him even in his dreams and was no less acute than the other thing that made him shudder: the fear of being buried alive. When his son left the country, he wrote to him in Polish. The fact that the replies he received from Fryderyk soon came from Paris and were signed Frédéric did nothing to change this; father and son continued to correspond in Polish about money and career matters, ill health, and the wretched situation in which Poland found itself.

Frédéric would never master French spelling and grammar. Even after having lived in Paris for several years he still spoke French with a strong accent. To make fun of his Slavic sibilants and rolling r's, George Sand tauntingly called him Frik-Frik or Chip-Chip. She was crazy about his soft lisping voice; he was as ashamed of his pronunciation as he was with a crease in the trousers to his dinner jacket.

In France, Chopin felt exiled from both his country and language, and that was no doubt the major reason why he sought refuge in Polish melodies and dance forms.

A similar situation existed for composers from Curaçao. Most of them were of European descent, from France (Blasini), Sweden (Palm), England (Corsen), Germany (Ulder), or Holland (Boskaljon), but they no longer spoke the language of their forebears. At home or in public they spoke Papiamentu or Spanish, seldom Dutch even though it was the official language of the island. A part of them was European due to their exposure to European civilization, while another part was a product of living at the threshold of South America. In Chopin they encountered the same sort of split personality.

Their admiration for the Pole no doubt had to do with the character his music exuded. Chopin was an elegant creature, if not as appealing to the ladies as I imagined him to be when as a nine-year-old I cut his picture out of a radio guide. On advertisements to promote his performances, they always printed Delacroix's portrait in which the composer is immortalized with those wild chestnut brown locks of hair, a sharp straight nose, and the brooding look of an introvert. In reality his hair was matted and colorless and he had a hooked nose, pouting lips, and timid-looking eyes without any lashes. His dandy image was an invention, intended to spread the spirit of romanticism. Notwithstanding, he did possess an inner refinement.

Chopin was reserved, proud, elegant, wistful, suddenly volatile and passionate, and then tranquil, closed, mysterious. He avoided women or sought refuge in impossible loves. Rejection was to be expected from the parents of the fifteen-year-old Maria Wodzinska, a young lady of noble birth in whom he was interested: he had no title and no money. When the inevitable rejection took place he slipped the letters from Maria in a folder and wrote on the cover in elegant calligraphy: "My Misfortune." Like a true romantic, he cultivated his grief; George Sand had to practically kidnap him, and when she finally did snare him, he did not want to share his bed with her right away. She won her suit by mothering him and nursing him on Majorca, where he fell gravely ill. Chopin inspired love, he seldom expressed it; he gave, as Liszt wrote, "everything except himself."

These were characteristics that matched the Caribbean temperament. Despite what the Dutch believe, Curaçaoans are neither crude nor ill mannered. Like true islanders they show a great deal of reservation at first toward foreigners. Even among themselves, they only show their true feelings with the greatest of difficulty; nowhere is the distance from the north to south shore very far, and on an island word gets around easily. In public they hide behind male pride or female respectability, but even more so through a show of exceptionally courteous manners. In familiar surroundings, the slightest incident is enough to trigger volatile displays of temper in no way inferior to that of the Latin American; yet their thoughts are just as easily distracted and they engage in the most heated debates with a faint smile on their faces. In fact, they are just as wistful as a sunset, and it is precisely this mood we hear in Chopin's plaintive harmonies.

In Western Europe, the mazurka was not granted a long life. After Chopin's death practically no composer dared try his hand at this dance form. The mazurka emigrated to Russia, where Tchaikovsky, Borodin, and Glinka indulged in it as the purest expression of the Slavic soul. Therefore Sergei Rachmaninov dedicated his 1894 mazurka to Tchaikovsky and not Chopin. The mazurka that formed the final movement of Rachmaninov's *Morceaux de Salon* was composed shortly after Tchaikovsky's death.

As far as I know Scriabin was the last Russian to compose an impressive series of mazurkas, written between 1888 and 1903. It was not until then that the mazurka began to become popular on the other side of the ocean. The dance was just as popular on Martinique and Guadeloupe as it was on Curaçao and Aruba; it was frequently a part of the concert repertoire in Cuba, Puerto Rico, and Santo Domingo from 1890 until well into the twentieth century. Both salon pianists and jazz orchestras performed mazurkas.

Chopin's influence could be heard throughout the Caribbean islands during the entire twentieth century, and his name lived on, from Havana to Kingston Town.

7

Which One of the Three?

Jules Blasini was probably the first person to bring Chopin sheet music to Curaçao. Chopin had already been dead for quite some time, but despite the triumphs he had celebrated in Paris, he had not had much luck with music publishers. It was partly his own fault: he had played them off against one another, hoodwinking them or branding them as Jews. They took a wait-and-see attitude until they could be certain that Chopin would prove a long-term success. It was not until 1860 that editions of his mazurkas, nocturnes, polonaises, scherzos, and ballads appeared in large numbers.

Jules Blasini (1847–1887) had been taking piano lessons from Jan Gerard Palm. When Blasini passed his entrance exam to the Paris Conservatory, the director sent a letter to his teacher Palm congratulating him on having supplied him with such an excellent student. The director seldom lavished such praise on one of his aspiring students, and the appeals commission worked overtime to process the huge number of applicants.

In the mid-nineteenth century, the Paris conservatory towered above any other music institute in Europe. Talented young people were admitted with just as much difficulty as Christians in Mecca. The conservatory statutes contained a clause that excluded foreigners from taking lessons. Exceptions were only made for those with exceptional talent. Father Offenbach went to a great deal of trouble to get his son, Jacques, a brilliant cellist, accepted. If the aspiring student came from the New World, he did not stand a ghost of a chance. Louis Moreau Gottschalk was not even allowed to audition; he had spent his childhood in New Orleans, and as the director said: "America is a land of steam engines."

It helped that Blasini's first and middle names were French: Jules François. He was assigned to the piano class taught by Georges

Mathias, a former student of Frédéric Chopin. He did not stick it out for long at the conservatory: he enrolled on 26 October 1865 and was struck off the enrollment list on 31 January 1866. He took private lessons and studied with opera composer Jules Massenet, the up-and-coming man of the day. It was not until eight years later that he returned to Curaçao.

At first I thought that Blasini was descended from an Italian Jewish family who had emigrated to Curaçao. At the beginning of the nineteenth century, a number of Jews from Venice had settled on the island, including the Capriles family (originally called Caprilli), whose offspring distinguished themselves throughout the nineteenth and twentieth centuries in quite a few disciplines, including medicine, psychiatry, trade, banking, and music. I suspected that Blasini's father had been among that group of Venetian Jews. However, pianist Livio Hermans, a great authority on Curaçaoan music, cast doubt on this when I asked him about it.

Indeed, the name Blasini is not included in the reference book *History of the Jews of the Netherlands Antilles*. Its authors, I. S. and S. A. Emmanuel, dedicated a separate chapter to the Jewish composers on Curaçao and only refer to Charles Maduro, Abraham Capriles, and Benjamin Namias de Castro. Nor does the name Blasini occur in the register of birth and deaths of the Jews on Curaçao from 1722 to 1830 that Krafft included in his *Historie en oude families van de Nederlandse Antillen* (History and Old Families of the Netherlands Antilles). That genealogical study did, however, provide another clue.

Slave owners received compensation from the government of the Netherlands after the abolition of slavery in 1863. In his book, Krafft published a list of those slave owners; on page 348 we read: "Invoice for compensation payments for the slaves on Curaçao. Jean Blasini for his s. 600 guilders."

Jean Blasini was Jules François's father. Two hundred guilders were paid for each slave set free. Jean Blasini lived in a small country estate, just outside the city limits, and had owned three slaves. Probably he was a Huguenot; quite a few Protestants who had fled France had settled in the West Indies, in Venezuela, Surinam, or in the Greater or Lesser Antilles. They kept their French first names—the father of the writer Cola Debrot, owner of Slagbaai, the biggest plantation on Bonaire, was named Jean Jacques, and his mother Marie Antoinette. Some of those French families had come to the Antilles via Antwerp and Middelburg, such as De Haseth, whose original name was De Hachette. Still others had fled from Saint-Domingue, including the families of Joubert and Perret Gentil. It is possible that Jean Blasini had belonged to that group of French who had sought refuge in Curaçao after the revolution led by Toussaint L'Ouverture. This would make it a lot easier to understand why his son Jules composed so many danzas, a style of music often performed in Saint-Domingue.

After consulting the two thick tomes of Hartog's history of Curaçao, I discovered the Blasinis had originally come from Corsica, which made it less probable they had been Huguenots since no Protestants were living there. Whatever his background, Jean Blasini settled on Curaçao in 1820. Within a short period of time, he had enough money at his disposal to buy three slaves. However, at the beginning of the nineteenth century a country estate was worth a pittance and most whites had at least five slaves, so he would not have amassed any great fortune.

Only the wealthiest families in the nineteenth century could afford to send their children to Europe to study. It is possible that Jules was given a place to stay by his relatives in Paris, with a Corsican aunt or uncle. But neither money nor relations helped the slightest bit when it came to being admitted to the conservatory. You had to be extremely talented—and exceptional talent was precisely what helped Jules get accepted. It must have been the case that his teacher Jan Gerard Palm had found a patron to finance his passage to France.

Once back on Curaçao, Blasini began composing. Only twenty of his works have survived. This is not just because he did not live long; it was the rule and not the exception for someone to die at forty-one in the days of tuberculosis and the galloping consumption. Many of his compositions must just have been lost. Blasini heralded the beginning of Dutch Antillean classical music, but in those pioneer days few works were filed away into archives. Livio Hermans found a few scores in Caracas; he suspects there are quite a few more to be found there. My own investigations have led to nothing; in Venezuela it is easier to find gold than printed paper.

We also do not know what he looked like; there are no drawings or paintings of Blasini in existence. According to oral tradition he was short and had a sharp facial features, but then so do all Corsicans. He did not marry, had no children, at least no legitimate ones. When he died no one felt the need to sort out or see to his personal belongings.

I first heard two of Blasini's compositions on the CD *Danza!* by Harold Martina, which was released in 1992. After studying at the Instituto de Bellas Artas in Medellín and the Music Academy in Vienna, Harold Martina (b. 1935) made a name for himself as a concert pianist in Colombia. Wherever he performed, he made it a point to propagate the music of his native island of Curaçao. He put it into a broader Caribbean perspective and always highlighted the similarities with other parts of the Antilles more than the differences. On the CD he plays dances of Jules Blasini alongside those by the Cubans Ignacio Cervantes and Ernesto Lecuona and the Colombian Louis Calvo, major nineteenth-century composers totally unknown in Europe.

The two works by his fellow countryman were called *Los ojitos de una Mexicana* and *¿Para cuál de las tres?* The titles betray the fact that Blasini was a womanizer. "Which One of the Three?" referred to a gentleman who frequently paid a call to the yellow ochre house in Otrobanda where the three unmarried sisters Estela, Josefina, and Elodia Chapman lived. Evidently he had an eye on one of these three young ladies, and all of Willemstad wondered which one of the three it was. Judging by the music itself, Blasini had no chance whatsoever with any of them; a deep melancholy resounds throughout the dance. It is a dreamy piece of music I heard at practically every party I went to in the years to come.

Blasini was an unrivalled Prince Charming. He did not charm just with his music; in Paris he had patiently observed how the ladies did their hair. Back in Willemstad his fingers conjured up towering hairdos. He was a frequent and highly sought-after guest in upper-class boudoirs, in which he not only touched the locks of hair, but shoulders and waists as well. The title of one of his cantatas alludes to this—*Adagio: Ne m'oubliez pas.*

Blasini had young Curaçaoans play mazurkas and waltzes during the many piano lessons he gave. Chopin's influence is clearly in evidence in the nocturne he composed. He found his own style in the dances in which he made use of the local rhythms. According to the prominent Curaçaoan pianist and composer Robert Rojer, they can only be played by a Curaçaoan; the *rubato* requires an extremely delicate touch down to the tenth of the measure. Toward the end of his life, Jules Blasini signed his compositions Julio Blasini. The half Frenchman had become fully Latin American.

It is also possible that it was Blasini's teacher Jan Gerard Palm (1831–1906) who introduced the works of Chopin on Curaçao. He lived a great deal longer than Blasini and composed more than a hundred miniature pieces, including six mazurkas and forty waltzes. Just where Jan Gerard Palm acquired his musical knowledge will always remain a mystery. In the waltz *El Sueño y el Triste Presente* he flew back and forth between the opposing musical themes with playful ease, and in the funeral march to commemorate Brion, the Curaçaoan general who had fought side by side with Simón Bolívar, he assimilated the latest trends from the Old World. Jan Gerard, who never left Curaçao, wanted to be called Gerry, pronounced the English way. He had been able to pilot his pupil Blasini into the Paris Conservatory thanks to a cunning letter of recommendation in impeccable French, and was in constant touch with Cuba, where the local phenomenon Gottschalk performed for packed houses.

Louis Moreau Gottschalk had been the most fanatic of all of Chopin's disciples. He carried his musical message throughout the Caribbean and even deep into the South American continent.

Gottschalk dressed like Chopin, cut his hair like Chopin, behaved like Chopin, and played the piano like Chopin: a virtuoso with fluency, gentleness, and a mastery of the use of the pedal.

8

Oh My Sweet Darling, Spare Me

Louis Moreau Gottschalk (1829–1869) spent the first years of his life in New Orleans, within hearing distance of Congo Square, where black musicians were given the exceptional privilege during the years of slavery of performing every Sunday afternoon in a frenzied atmosphere.

His mother, Aimeé Brusle, was a Cajun from Louisiana, his father a German Jew who had immigrated at a young age to America from London, where his parents had sought their fortune.

Aimée spoke French at home and could not read English. Her ancestors had exchanged Louisiana in the middle of the eighteenth century for Saint-Domingue, and forty-five years later, after the declaration of the black republic, came back to the United States by way of Jamaica. At first they had not disapproved of the slave revolt; Gottschalk was named after his uncle Moreau Bruslé, who for a short time had been the revolutionary leader Toussaint L'Ouverture's secretary.

So on his mother's side he clearly had ties to Haiti, which he even referred to as "a mysterious affinity." His father imported goods from Bremen and Hamburg but earned considerably more in the slave trade. In New Orleans Edward Gottschalk supported two families from the proceeds, the official one with Aimée, and the illegitimate one with Judith Françoise Rubio, a so-called free woman of color, whose forebears, like Aimée's, had come from Saint-Domingue. He had seven children with the first and four with the latter. He recognized all eleven of them, which caused him to be in constant need of money.

Louis Moreau was not very fond of his father. He refused to learn German and on his later travels he avoided going to Germany and England. He did, however, absolutely adore his Creole mother, which he expressed in countless compositions and which he would always convey in the way he spoke English: a little like Hercule Poirot in Agatha Christie films.

Edward Gottschalk pushed his son into music, with the singular aim of making money. Edward could not read a single note of music but had read in the newspaper that child prodigies were making fortunes. He invested in his son like real estate, and when the young man became famous, he came to collect the money he felt he was entitled to as some kind of landlord would.

Louis Moreau took piano lessons, violin lessons, and composition from the age of seven; when he was twelve he was sent to further his musical studies at the Paris Conservatory, where Blasini had also studied. That did not happen, however: as an American he did not stand a ghost of a chance to be admitted, and he lacked the extraordinary letter that had led to Blasini's admission; all he could do was take private lessons from Camille Stamaty, a student of Felix Mendelssohn Bartholdy. Besides Gottschalk, Stamaty was molding another talent, Camille Saint-Saëns, in a ruthless but efficient way: Saint-Saëns was soon regarded a child prodigy. A month before his sixteenth birthday Louis Moreau made his debut in the Salle Pleyel, on April 2, 1845.

Among his audience was Sigismund Thalberg, "the man with the iron wrists." The Viennese pianist was a great rival in Paris at the time with Liszt and Chopin and won the battle of the virtuosos according to the taste of his contemporaries, which left Chopin indifferent and Liszt furious. Thalberg discovered in the young Gottschalk a new challenger.

In the first row sat Chopin himself. The constantly shivering Pole had come to listen to the performance of his piano composition in E-minor. Afterward he rushed to the soloist's dressing room. According to Gottschalk's first biographer he said in a languid voice: *"Bien, mon enfant, bien, très bien, donnez-moi encore la main."*

No, claimed Gottschalk's French music publisher later, Chopin had said: *"Embrassez-moi, encore, encore!"* Not true, said Gottschalk's sister Clara afterwards; Chopin had laid his hand on the boy's head to give him his paternal blessing: "*Je prédis que vous serez le roi des pianists.*"

Gottschalk would indeed become the king of the pianists, in New Orleans, New York, Cuba, Puerto Rico, Martinique, Peru, Chile, Argentina, Uruguay, and Brazil. He gave thousands of performances to audiences who were sometimes so ecstatic they carried him on their shoulders to his hotel where they cheered him deep into the night. He often had to bid a final farewell to his admirers from the balcony of his hotel with a majestic bow.

As a composer he introduced countless Creole rhythms, in the exact same spirit as Chopin and Liszt, who had brought Polish and Hungarian dances to the world's attention. Gottschalk became familiar with Creole music through his mother, his childhood nanny Sally, who had been born in Saint-Domingue, and by his grandmother, who had spent the first thirty years of her life there as well. He had heard *La Belle Lolotte* sung at home, and used the theme to it for his *La Savane*; at home he had also heard *En avan'Grenadie* and used the melody for *La Bananier*; at home he had seen Sally dance to the beat of *Quan'patate la cuite*, the melody of which he used in his most famous composition *Bamboula*.

He wrote his *Pasquinade* in 1860, the first piece that prefigured ragtime eight years before Scott Joplin was born and thirty-nine years before the *Maple Leaf Rag* appeared in print. He was a forerunner to Joplin, Gershwin, Ives, Carter, and Ellington, drove American music toward swing, and would nevertheless end up being forgotten in his land of birth.

South of New Orleans his legacy is much deeper. You can hear his influence in practically every Caribbean composition that followed. He set to work on the mazurka, and transformed the polka and the contradanse until they were more reminiscent of waving palm trees than rustling birches.

Gottschalk's early mazurkas were strongly influenced by Chopin, but he quickly gave them a Creole twist, and in his later works combined the piano techniques of Chopin and Thalberg with Caribbean motifs. In formal terms his etude *Madeleine*, which he composed in Rio de Janeiro, fits seamlessly with Chopin's etudes, but sounds like a Latin American bolero.

In the end, Gottschalk shared with his musical model the fact that he died just before the age of forty. During a concert in Rio de Janeiro when he was performing his composition *Morte* he fell forward on the grand piano. His death throes lasted another three weeks, and because of the hassles with payments of outstanding debts, nine months went by before he could be buried in New York. On his tombstone would be engraved the words L.M. GOTTSCHALK—MORTE, thus feeding the myth that Gottschalk had forced his own death, in a similar way to Mozart, who died after having committed the first sections of his *Requiem* to paper. The *e* in *Morte* indicated that Gottschalk had written the piece for a woman; *morte* refers to the poem by Victor Hugo that begins with: *Elle est morte.*

Upwards of three hundred Gottschalk compositions have survived. They are almost all miniatures. In this he was also a forerunner to the Caribbean composers that followed, who seldom if ever dared to write compositions on a grand scale. Among his pieces that usually lasted four, five, or six minutes were quite a few contradanses, which Gottschalk called "Cuban dances."

His melodies are quite tuneful, as attested to by *Oh! Ma Charmante, Epargnez-moi* which I heard for the first time on the CD by Harold Martina. Martina quite rightly opens his compilation of dance pieces with three works by Gottschalk, to indicate he stood at the cradle of Caribbean music, or to put it even more forcefully, that he actually created it and brought it to life.

Oh! My Sweet Darling, Spare Me sounds like a song without lyrics—a gorgeous song you can listen to over and over again and still be moved every time. Gottschalk was not so much a womanizer as he was willing prey to women. His hooked nose, high forehead, and tousled hair made him resemble Chopin, at least in the way Delacroix portrayed him. Wherever Gottschalk appeared he was besieged by women. The young pianist Amy Fay was one of them; once she had come of age she admitted she had a "silly infatuation" with him "just like 99,999 other American girls" and that, despite her gray hair, he "is still present in her heart." After giving a concert, like a pop star Gottschalk had to retreat to the sanctuary of his dressing room—hence his *Oh! My Sweet Darling, Spare Me*. But when the ravishing Irène de los Ríos y Noguerida, for whom the piece was intended, ran away from him, leaving Cuba in a rush, he composed the deeply sad *Adios a la Havana.*

That piece too only lasts a few minutes. Still, Gottschalk did not always choose to compose short pieces; he wrote three operas, and for a performance in the Tacón Theater in Havana he asked for sixty-eight clarinets, forty-eight violins, twenty-nine French horns, thirty-three tubas, thirty-eight trombones, forty-five drums, two triangles, and one hundred and ninety-eight singers. The fact that his request was honored immediately is ample testament to just how popular he was.

In the course of his travels Gottschalk may have visited Curaçao, though he never performed there. His greatest triumphs were in Havana, Puerto Rico, Lima, Montevideo, Rio de Janeiro, and Saint-Pierre, the capital of Martinique, which would vanish under yards of ash and stone after the infamous volcanic eruption of Mont Pelée in 1902. His work was performed on Curaçao by its own music pioneers Jan Gerard Palm, Chris Ulder, Jules Blasini, and Joseph Sickman Corsen, perhaps a little too often: a reviewer praised one young pianist who "finally got out of the rut of always playing Gottschalk."

He sank into oblivion in the twentieth century, even in the islands of the Caribbean. In 1983 Wim Statius Muller released an album called *Antillean Dances opus 2.* He got rave reviews and musicologist David Dubal called him "the Antillean Gottschalk" on WQXR, the classical radio station owned by the *New York Times.* However, Statius Muller had to remind himself just who Gottschalk was.

Since then he has browsed Gottschalk's oeuvre. He thinks some of his compositions are quite good, such as *Bamboula, Oh ma belle,* and the mazurkas and Cuban dances. That, however, does not mitigate his general opinion of him: "Gottschalk also wrote a lot of junk." They may indeed have sounded much better in Gottschalk's own renditions of them. When it comes to a score by Gottschalk, the words of Rubinstein about Rachmaninov come to mind: "Whenever I hear Rachmaninov being played, I always think: a good composer. Whenever I hear Rachmaninov play his own works, I think: what a great composer."

9

The Virtuoso Nomad

I discovered Gottschalk at an opportune moment. American historian S. Frederick Starr's substantial biography *Bamboula! The Life and Times of Louis Moreau Gottschalk* was published in 1995, followed in 1996 by the just as detailed *Louis Moreau Gottschalk et son temps* by the Canadian sociologist Réginald Hamel. They were certainly not the first biographies—when he was alive Gottschalk had already been adulated twice in book form, and before he sank into oblivion he would be the subject of no less than four hagiographies—but these were the first academic works on his life. The books complement each other wonderfully: Starr places Gottschalk in the American search for cultural identity, while Hamel approaches him from a Creole perspective. In that same decade, French pianist Georges Rabol, the son of a black musician from Martinique, recorded two CDs with works by Gottschalk, and the Irishman Philip Martin went a step further by recording all the piano works by Gottschalk still in existence on a total of seven CDs between 1990 and 2004.

I was able to read about and listen to Gottschalk, and to be honest, I was in for a bit of a surprise. Not that he was the misunderstood genius; I had to agree with Wim Statius Muller that sometimes Gottschalk set low standards for himself and was incapable of throwing total or partial failures into the wastepaper basket. Nevertheless, he had just as often infused his music with a contagious feeling of euphoria, and I became fond of Gottschalk, of the man himself, the traveler, the phenomenon.

First and foremost, Gottschalk was a nomad. He stayed in each country he visited for several months and sometimes even years, with the sole purpose of acquiring new experiences. He enjoyed the company of poets, writers, and journalists just as much as composers and musicians; he accepted the invitations of five presidents, from high-minded democrats such as Abraham Lincoln to bloodthirsty dictators such as Vernacio Flores in Montevideo, wandering through their palaces like dazed madmen. Gottschalk wanted to see everything with his own eyes and hear everything with his own ears in order to be able to process it into music or writing. He sent reportage-like written impressions to the French magazine *La France musicale* from every country he visited for a long period of time. The magazine sold these pieces on to newspapers in Milan, Mainz, Madrid, and St. Petersburg, and gradually Gottschalk gained the reputation in Europe of being a nomadic virtuoso. All his articles were posthumously collected under title *Notes d'un pianiste*, and in 1964 when they were republished by the New York publisher Knopf, it enabled a reviewer to sneer: "If Gottschalk did not deserve fame for his music, then at least he did for these travel stories."

The nineteenth century prescribed that composers lead deeply tragic lives. Hector Berlioz tried to make an exception to the rule; like Gottschalk he was intensely curious and put his impressions down in writing. However, when it came to his music he was generally underestimated. Gottschalk was spared that sad fate; he was worshipped his entire life. Given his cheerful disposition, he adhered to one of the lines of the Cuban poet Manuel Ramírez: "*vivir es gozar, amar es vivir*" (to live is to enjoy, to love is to live). As far as that was concerned he had a great deal in common with Rossini, who indeed embraced him as a kindred spirit.

Sometimes he was short of cash, sometimes his intestines bothered him due to the umpteenth change of climate and diet, and sometimes he was almost hooked by a woman, such as the American journalist and writer Ada Clare, who claimed that Gottschalk was the father of her son. Whether or not she was right, was never determined; in any case she wrote a scandalous *roman à clef* about him in the same vein as George Sand about Chopin or Marie d'Agoult about Liszt, and Gottschalk considered it wiser to take his leave. From that moment on he chose only to make eyes at young girls, pretty enough to court but of an age too tender to deflower. He inhaled the odor of the mademoiselles, and when they turned his head, he quickly lit a Cuban cigar.

Gottschalk sought adoration, not sex, which made him practically the only nineteenth-century artist not to have contracted a venereal disease. Nevertheless, in California he became embroiled in a sex scandal. He and a friend picked up two fourteen-year-old girls from a boarding school in the middle of the night, and due to a slip-up failed to bring them back before the morning roll call. Gottschalk was threatened with being indicted for obscene conduct with underage minors. He escaped going to trial by sailing to Peru under an assumed name.

Every once in a while he suffered from the consequences of his popularity, though most of the time he bore his fate of being an idol in a lighthearted manner. His fame allowed him to indulge in any crazy whim he desired. In New Orleans he became acquainted with a balloonist. He immediately wanted to take to the sky with the aeronaut and for six minutes they hovered above the city. The balloon suddenly started descending at a dangerous speed, skimming past a factory chimney and just missing a steam locomotive pulling out of a railway station. Any right-minded person living in the nineteenth century would never have dreamed of repeating such a futuristic piece of daredevilry. Gottschalk again clambered into the balloon the next day, taking a harmonium with him where he composed a short piece high in the sky that he called *l'Extase*.

In that era music was a serious business, not at all to be taken lightly. Gottschalk was the first to dare to be lighthearted.

No sooner had he come of age than he attracted public attention with four lively pieces of music called *Le Bananier, Bamboula, Le Mancenillier,* and *La Savane. La Bananier* was subtitled *chanson nègre,* and the entire Parisian cultural elite turned out to hear that "black song" performed. Listening to Gottschalk himself playing *La Bananier* in the salon of newspaper magnate Emile Garardin were no less than Lamartine, Victor Hugo, Théophile Gautier, and Alexandre Dumas. Sixty years before the advent of jazz, the poets and novelists were given a foretaste and were absolutely thrilled. They were amazed at so much rhythm, such exuberance, and their response was one of elation. From that point onward Gottschalk was known as *Gottschalk de Louisiana* and his reputation was established. He immediately embarked on a tour to cash in on his fame.

If you listen to his compositions in chronological order, you can tag along on all the journeys Gottschalk undertook. Wherever he went, he was inspired by the local musicians. His first trip was to

Spain. He stayed there for two years, learned to speak fluent Spanish, and composed *Minuit à Sevilla* and *Chanson de Gitano*, pieces reminiscent of the early works of De Falla or Granados, and which could have easily been included in Bizet's *Carmen*—except it would be another fifty years before De Falla and Granados started composing and twenty-five years before *Carmen* premiered in Paris. The amazing thing about these pieces is that Gottschalk combined Iberian motifs with the style of Chopin, especially his mazurkas. Wherever he went, Gottschalk absorbed musical impressions without forgetting his master.

Gottschalk had an exceptional gift for making contacts. In every country he composed a large-scale showpiece, which he performed with the help of local musicians. He began in Spain, where he composed *Siege of Saragossa* for ten pianos. He played the most demanding part himself; the other nine were played by local pianists. He bonded with the musicians during rehearsals, often resulting in the start of a friendship; after the performance he was a welcome guest in salons and artist associations. All other traveling virtuosos remained outsiders; Gottschalk crawled like lice on a dog.

Naturally, from time to time this caused professional envy. In Spain the court pianist slammed the door of a coach so hard it broke the virtuoso's right pinky finger. Gottschalk made light of the incident, claiming that a medical student had shook his hand too firmly. That student was purportedly jealous of Gottschalk having made overtures to a nightclub singer from Madrid by the name of Carmen. The first version of the incident is probably the truth; Gottschalk put his own spin on the story in order not to spoil his good relations with the Spanish court.

In Havana he again performed his *Siege of Saragossa* with nine Cuban pianists. That performance in the Gran Teatro de Tacón brought him into contact with the grand master of the Cuban contradanza, the completely self-effacing composer Manuel Saumell (1817–1870). The Cuban writer Natalio Galán compared the meeting to that of "Buxtehude with Bach." I considered that utter nonsense when I read it in Starr's biography; it was not until a few months later that I heard pianist Georges Rabol's recordings of four Saumell pieces. The four songs *La Tedezca, La niña bonita, Recuerdos tristes,* and *La Matalide* lasted less than five minutes between them. What

Saumell does in those works, which he wrote around 1850, bordered on the incredible. All of a sudden I realized where Gottschalk had gotten his rhythms from; it was as if I were listening to a work by Scott Joplin, Jelly Roll Morton, Artie Matthews, or some other ragtime composer, or a contradanse by a Curaçaoan composer from the early twentieth century, or—even more modern—to passages from Gershwin's *Spanish Prelude*. Saumell was the first to slip Afro-Cuban rhythms underneath melody lines in the style of Schubert and Chopin, and the talented Gottschalk realized immediately how effective such a combination could be. After meeting Saumell he threw himself into Cuban contradanzas and his own rhythms took on the syncopated intensity that later came to be described as "typical Gottschalk." Gottschalk stole, and in turn was plundered by others himself. For his *Carmen*, Bizet used the *habanera* rhythm from *Minuit à Seville*—he had a considerable collection of Gottschalk's sheet music—and the Antillean composers went to town with his Cuban dances.

In the northeast of the United States, where the old misunderstanding was still very much alive and kicking, the critics had an aversion to Gottschalk. Being light-footed and lighthearted was equated with being lazy and banal. The fiercest resistance came from Boston, where all classical music was measured by German musical standards. Gottschalk was not in the same league as Beethoven; besides, he had been educated in France and preferred to perform with the likes of Italian opera singers and divas. It took Gottschalk many years to conquer the "civilized" United States of America, and in the end he prevailed, not because of his music, but because of his political stance.

Without the slightest bit of hesitation he supported the Union during the American Civil War. His Southern roots did not keep him from considering slavery to be a backward-looking, degrading practice, since the movement to secede from the Union had been predicated upon maintaining slavery. The South, he wrote in one of his notes, "is intent on destroying one of the finest political moments of modern times—namely the American Union, in the name of slavery." To give his intentions musical expression, he composed a piece called *The Union*, which yielded him an invitation to play for President Lincoln and his wife. He told reporters that he had freed three slaves in New Orleans. It was a publicity stunt; he had never owned slaves.

The standpoint he took had more to do with his antipathy for his father, the trader who scoured markets for bargain deals. In Paris Gottschalk would not have failed to notice that Victor Schoelcher was a regular guest at the salons where Chopin performed. Schoelcher, the most vociferous advocate for the abolition of slavery (and the French Assistant Secretary who signed the 1848 decree for French abolition of slavery), was a personal friend of Chopin—and of Liszt, as well as the piano manufacturer Camille Pleyel. For Chopin the fate of black slaves was the same as the serfs in Russian-occupied Poland. He had a soft spot in his heart for Schoelcher, certainly since this champion of human rights came from the upper middle class—his father owned a porcelain factory in the Alsace—and he was a man of impeccable manners. Whenever Pleyel travelled to Guyana, Cuba, and the French Antilles, he attended to Schoelcher's business by chronicling the horrors of slavery he encountered in a series of reports. Those who Gottschalk admired the most, Chopin first and foremost, but also Camille Pleyel, at whose salon he made his debut, were appalled at the practices his father had been guilty of all his life. And so Gottschalk did not waver a single moment fifteen years later when he came down on the side of the abolitionists versus the anti-abolitionists; he believed he still had to do something to make amends to Chopin, Liszt, and Pleyel.

The Civil War had a detrimental effect on the quality of his work. He wrote such tearjerkers as *The Last Hope* and *The Dying Poet* to commemorate the fallen; he increasingly became the entertainer with politically correct sentiments and the wrong kind of music. During the first months of 1862 he gave one hundred and nine concerts in one hundred and twenty days. The twenty thousand kilometers he travelled in trains amid drunken soldiers did nothing to make him any happier, although he cheerfully informed his European readers that "Yankees are certainly the world's only real travellers." He described Sundays in Boston as "*ennui, ennui, ennui,*" and the northern Protestantism all around him as "concentrated boredom." He yearned for the South, for the warmth and hospitality and the delirious singing in most of the churches.

Back in Cuba, life again smiled upon him. He entitled a danza he had just written *Di que sí*, and a day later his friend Manuel Saumell wrote one in reply calling it *Di que no*. In the pious Northeast he had felt it necessary to compose a religious, meditative piece; in Havana they were always in for a good lark. The city had the cluttered charm of New Orleans and the prominence of Paris. Thanks to the sugar industry Havana was one of the world's most prosperous cities. Gottschalk felt at home there; he began his day with a cup of pitch black coffee at the Café Louvre, then wandered into a working-class neighborhood to immerse himself in the Creole rhythms and listen to percussion groups playing *tumba francesa*. Back in his hotel room he composed such little gems such as *Ojos Criollos*, in which you can hear his footsteps as well as the joyful flute and drumming that had caught his ear.

It now seems completely natural: the classically trained Gottschalk's ears catch the Afro-Caribbean rhythms, which he then assimilates into his music. Daring? We can scarcely believe it. All you have to do is read interviews with Duke Ellington to get an idea of the prejudices that were involved. Long after the heyday of the Cotton Club, in 1940 the Duke was asked straight out why he allowed himself to be inspired by "jungle drumming and howling." For the straight-laced, jazz appealed to the basest instincts in the underbelly; by then Gottschalk's composition *Creole Eyes* was already eighty years old.

After a tour that took him to all the cities and towns of Cuba, Gottschalk travelled to Puerto Rico, where he became acquainted with the local *bomba* and danza. On Christmas Eve he witnessed the annual procession of the *jíbaros*, the peasant farmers from Puerto Rico. The next day he composed *Souvenir de Porto-Rico*, one of the loveliest Caribbean compositions of the nineteenth century, full of *tresillo* and *cinquillo* rhythms that rise to a crescendo before suddenly descending into a final lyrical adagio.

Gottschalk enjoyed rural life in Puerto Rico. He spent several months in plantation houses, did not pass up a single party, and tickled the ivories of every piano in any village fortunate enough to have one. Right before one of his performances in a country inn, one of the guests suddenly died. Because Gottschalk would be leaving the next day, the innkeeper insisted on letting the concert take place, even though it meant playing in the hall where the deceased lay in state. A stage was built that arched over the coffin on which a grand piano was placed. That evening, Gottschalk played variations on local songs and dances. The audience egged him on. He banged harder and harder on the keys; he pushed his feet deeper and deeper into the pedals. Then the piano crashed through the floor. The audience rushed over to him screaming: "He's dead." A second later Gottschalk scrambled to his feet above the coffin to a deafening volley of laughter.

The next islands Gottschalk visited were Jamaica, Barbados, and Trinidad. After a stay in Guyana and Suriname, he wanted to travel onward to Venezuela, but there was a civil war in progress, so he went to Martinique and Guadeloupe. On the latter island he retreated into the mountains for several months, settling near the smoking volcano La Soufrière, with a mentally retarded servant who read Voltaire and Rousseau and was a virtuoso on the violin. In the dispatches he sent to European newspapers, he made Guadeloupe out to be some practically uninhabited island and himself as some Robinson Crusoe and the mulatto servant Firmin Moras into his man Friday. Moras, who could hardly speak, would stay by his side until the day Gottschalk died.

Living like a hermit, Gottschalk intended on getting down to some serious work on a grand scale. It turns out he did indeed compose a symphony, though no more than a few sketches have survived. Due to his travelling existence he lost quite a few pieces of luggage and compositions, and after his death in Rio de Janeiro an unscrupulous impresario made off with several of his scores. Some works resurfaced on the black market; quite a few were lost forever.

Back in Cuba, he organized a monster concert in which four hundred and fifty musicians took part, both professionals and amateurs. His orchestra included Afro-Cuban rhythm instruments, from the lowliest shakers to gigantic drums. At the last minute he added forty pianists to the four hundred and fifty performers. The concert was a real happening; everyone and anyone in Havana who could play a few notes participated. The reviewers wrote that music could not sound any grander or more powerful. Gottschalk merely took it as a challenge: for the monster concert he organized years later in Rio de

Janeiro, he invited no less than six hundred and fifty musicians. He enlisted the services of brass bands of the Brazilian army and navy, two German orchestras, seventy music teachers, and the orchestra of a local revue theatre. He put eleven copyists to work around the clock for a week to write out the scores for all the musicians.

During his travels, Gottschalk passed on the knowledge he had acquired in Europe. He gave lessons in New York to the Venezuelan Teresa Carreño (1853–1917), who would become one of the most prominent concert pianists at the turn of the century. In 1886 she performed in Curaçao and, as always, began her recital with her own composition entitled *Gottschalk March*. The young Arthur Rubenstein saw her play in Berlin thirteen years later, a Valkyrie-like appearance "with the power and turbulence of two men." In Cuba Gottschalk took the young Ignacio Cervantes (1849–1905) under his wing, in Chile Federico Guzmán (1837–1885), and in Brazil Brasilio Itibere de Cunha (1846–1913). Cervantes would turn into Cuba's greatest nineteenth-century composer, Guzmán the greatest Chilean composer, and Itibere de Cunha would be the man who paved the way for Villa-Lobos. Gottschalk took up a collection from his audiences in order for Guzmán to further his studies in Paris. And to each pupil he gave his dearest, most precious memory: the delicate, reserved, and sensitive performance of Chopin in a Parisian salon. He was not to be compared with Liszt, whom he had also heard in Paris and whom he reproached as having "an insatiable thirst for fame"—a little like the sort of criticism one high flyer gives another.

In Lima, he reverted to organizing simpler concerts for ten pianos. In Peru he was inspired by the local *zamacuecas* and listened intently to the *tristos* or Indian flute.

He travelled seven hundred kilometers into the interior of the country on the back of a donkey. These sojourns were not without danger: Gottschalk never forgot to take his pistol with him nor his walking stick, which sheathed a hidden sword. He regularly was forced to pull his gun, and with his walking stick he successfully warded off an assailant, though not in some obscure backlands but in Buenos Aires; and the man who attacked him was a drunken Frenchman. South America gave him plenty to write about—from the darkened recesses of his lodgings he spied on the rebels on horseback in Lima, and he survived a cholera epidemic in Buenos

Aires that claimed the lives of tens of thousands of victims—but in musical terms he had reached the end of his tether. His interest in native melodies and rhythms faded. Cuba, Puerto Rico, Martinique, and Guadeloupe had made an impression on him, since the local music constantly reminded him of his grandmother, mother, and his nanny's roots in Saint-Domingue. In Argentina he used local rhythms that foreshadowed the tango in his compositions *Dernier amour* and *Souvenir de Buenos Aires,* though in Brazil he was not at all taken with the local rhythms. In Chile he listened intently to the *mecapaqueña;* in Uruguay, where quite a few German colonists had settled, he studied the scores of Wagner.

"New, admirable, picturesque, outrageously distinguished," were the terms he used to describe Wagner's music in his *Notes,* and this made him think it was time to return to Europe and head for Germany. It was the land of his father, after all, "and France in recent years had no more to offer than Offenbach and champagne"; and he had reached the age at which he had been able to put the frustrations of childhood behind him. In preparation for his impending trip to Germany he wrote a couple of *Lieder.* A case of food poisoning put an abrupt end to his plans; the poisoning led to an inflammation of the appendix, and since it went untreated, to a case of peritonitis. The Brazilian emperor Dom Carlos II had him rushed to the mountains, but the fresh air did little more than ease his suffering.

Gottschalk directed his last words to the administering physician. "I have travelled much and have often been dangerously ill but never have I found a friend as devoted as you. A father or brother could not have done more. Your efforts are truly superhuman." He made the sign of the cross, kissed the doctor's hand, and drew his last breath.

A gentleman to the last.

Had he lived longer he would have become a universal composer. His untimely death limited his influence on Caribbean music, but indeed gave it form and direction. Joseph Sickman Corsen understood this all too well. When the first theatre was opened on Curaçao in 1872, he played Gottschalk's *Souvenir de Porto-Rico.* The applause was just as thunderous as it had been in Havana, when after a performance Gottschalk was showered under a mass of women's hats, and three hundred and fifty bouquets.

10

An Island of Defaulters

In 1886 Curaçao boasted seven composers with a population of no more than twenty-six thousand souls. By the start of the twentieth century their number had tripled. The printing presses of music publishers Librería A. Bethencourt e Hijos rolled from early in the morning until sunset. Composers from Willemstad, Venezuela, Puerto Rico, and Santo Domingo all had their musical scores printed there either by Imprenta Capriles or Tipografía Excelsior.

The local composers lived on an insignificant rock sixty-one kilometers long and eleven kilometers wide, and were in seventh heaven. They could choose from no less than three music publishers who were all keen to acquire new works. Chopin had to hawk his wares all his life and a third of his work was never published. And he lived in the cultural capital of the world.

Don Agustín Bethencourt laid the basis for publishing music on Curaçao. Born in 1826 in Santa Cruz de Tenerife, at the age of fourteen he decided to try his luck in the New World and exchanged the Canary Islands for Venezuela. He became merchant, teacher, justice of the peace, and pharmacist—the nineteenth-century man could still have all this on his plate in the vast country that was Venezuela, which had in common with the Wild West that it lay waiting with open arms for new settlers to arrive. In Valencia he had presumably already started printing pamphlets and lampoons; in any case he learned how to print. After nineteen years of residence he had to suddenly flee for political reasons. He sailed to Curaçao, taking in Willemstad's ambience while waiting there for a ship to take him back to Santa Cruz de Tenerife—lighthearted, hard-working, free, for whites at least. Bethencourt was as white as his Norman forefathers, who had settled large areas of the Canary Islands. He mingled easily in the company of Huguenots and Jews who ruled the roost in Curaçao, and he did not have to learn another language to make himself understood. He rented a store, began importing sheet music from Schonberger Musique in Paris, and quickly established his own bookstore and music publishing house.

The short, stocky Bethencourt, who in Willemstad was given the nickname *Papa Anchu* (Fat Daddy), coupled his business acumen with an unselfish love of music. He gathered a circle of young musicians and poets around him, calling it the *Groupe des Six*, some fifty years before a similar group was formed in Paris with the same name. Three of them were Jews: David Salas, Haim de Abraham Senior, and David Mendes Chumaceiro; the three others, Joseph Sickman Corsen, Ernesto Römer, and Adolfo Wolfschoon, were Catholics and had a great affinity with Latin America. Bethencourt was an ardent amateur cellist who founded the first string quartet on Curaçao, and who conducted a symphony orchestra he founded, calling it the Academia de Música. He just as ardently threw himself into dance music, which he performed in an ensemble. He brought music instructors over to Curaçao from Venezuela, including the composer Felipe Larrazábal, founder of the conservatory in Caracas, who also had to seek a safe haven for political reasons. On Curaçao he composed the intensely melancholic *Plegaria del Proscrito*—Prayer for an Exile. Exiles from Venezuela, Colombia, and Santo Domingo came and went in Bethencourt's house.

Papa Anchu started the advertiser *Boletín Comercial* that would develop into Curaçao's first newspaper, published stacks of music scores, and laid the foundations for what was to become *Notas y Letras*, which he founded in 1886. He died suddenly just before the first issue was about to appear, and at his funeral it looked as though the entire Curaçaoan music scene was about to vanish into his grave. "I am afraid that when the final stone has been laid to rest on this coffin, it will also be the first stone to be thrown against the building of our musical culture," said Dr. David Capriles, a passionate amateur musician.

Without Bethencourt's efforts, Antillean waltzes and mazurkas would have died a premature death. He created the platform; he gave young Dutch Antillean composers the chance to develop. *Notas y Letras* made popular Jules Blasini's dance music in Puerto Rico, and Chris Ulder and Julia Moreno's waltzes in Peru.

The poet/musician/composer Joseph Sickman Corsen (1853–1911) was the editor-in-chief of *Notas y Letras*. He was assisted by Haim de Abraham Senior, who did the layout, typesetting, and proofreading. Haim Senior had plenty of experience, owned his own printing establishment, Tipografía Excelsior, and published a literary magazine. The third editor was a Spanish teacher by the name of Ernesto Römer, who wrote editorials, solicited material from writers, poets, and political exiles, and canvassed subscribers.

Corsen was the boss. On his father's side he was descended from the Irish-English merchant John Corser, who had arrived on Curaçao at the end of the eighteenth century. Corser could not have come at a better moment in time: after the French had occupied the Netherlands and declared the Batavian Republic, the English saw their chance and occupied Curaçao. John Corser became a confidant of the British governor, which certainly did not do him any financial harm as a merchant in food articles.

The news that Napoleon Bonaparte had been defeated at Waterloo reached Curaçao two months after the fact, and the results of the Congress of Vienna, which again redrew colonial boundaries and gave back the islands of Curaçao, Bonaire, Aruba, Saba, Sint Eustatius, and a part of St. Martin to the former owner, the Netherlands, did not take place until the end of that year, as a result of which the English did not leave Curaçao until 1816.

In the meantime, John Corser became a prosperous man and had no intention of leaving. His son James Dutchified the family name into Corsen (or did not protest when the civil servant at the municipal registry changed the *r* into an *n*); his grandson Daniel left his business to his brothers and established himself as a piano teacher. Joseph Sickman received his first piano lessons from his father, Daniel, so systematically that he was able to perform in public at the age of thirteen. He performed a piano concerto with the Academia de Música—in all probability a work of Mozart.

On his mother's side, Joseph hailed from the Sickman family in the province of Zeeland in the Netherlands. The name was in danger of dying out; in order to prevent that from happening all future Corsen generations were given the Christian name Sickman, a convention widely used by colonists. The connection to the German family Ulder was just as strong. Daniel Corsen and Chris Ulder were half brothers; they had the same mother. This was of paramount importance to Joseph's upbringing; besides his father he also received lessons from his Uncle Chris, who was the organist in the synagogue, bandmaster of the civic guard, and one of the first full-time composers in Curaçao.

Just like all children from well-to-do families on Curaçao, Joseph was sent to a private Spanish school, the Colegio León or Colegio Bazalt, and after elementary school he was taught at home by his father and a few private tutors. It was not until 1873 that the local authorities passed a law that allowed the founding of special schools; it would take until the turn of the century before friars built the first Catholic schools. Parents, aunts, and uncles largely determined the extent of a child's general education. Daniel Corsen had a bookcase full of French literature, taught his son French, and developed his mathematical skills on a par with European high school students. Uncle Chris Ulder brushed up his German and familiarized him with Central European music, with Haydn, Mozart, Schubert, the German romantics, the young Beethoven, and Mendelssohn. Joseph learned the Iberian repertoire, having spent a few years in Venezuela as a young man.

There are several gaps in Corsen's life story, even though his granddaughter's husband, Fons Rutten, scrutinized every archive he could find looking for material about the composer and the poet. We still do not know, for instance, what Corsen actually did in Venezuela; Rutten was unable to find out whether he worked or studied there. Nevertheless, thanks to his short biography, which he managed to glean thanks to years of tireless research, we have evidence to show that the Corsen family had completely assimilated. Joseph spoke Papiamentu at home, Spanish on the street. He availed himself solely of Dutch when he translated verse by the nineteenth-century Dutch poets Tollens, Bilderdijk, and Rhijnvis Feith. His first poems were written in Spanish and later ones in Papiamentu; most of his music reviews were written in Spanish for *Notas y Letras*. Corsen never travelled to Europe, knowing it only through literature. He translated Borger's poem "Aan de Rijn" (On the Rhine) into Spanish to be able to imagine what the river actually looked like.

His compositions reveal that he was just as familiar with Chopin and Schubert as he was with Spanish dances and Venezuelan folk music. After his stay on the South American continent—"the other shore," as they call it on Curaçao—he travelled to Aruba. In those days that was an uncommon thing to do; the strong currents in the channels between the islands constantly hindered shipping traffic. It was much easier to sail to Venezuela from Curaçao than it was from Curaçao to Aruba or Bonaire; the distance between the islands remained great and would only disappear definitely once air traffic had become commonplace. On Aruba Corsen listened to the *joropos* by the Venezuelan immigrants, and he married Margaretha Federica Ponson. Her dark eyes led one to suspect she had Native American blood in her veins.

Back in Curaçao the Corsen family moved into a house in the Pietermaai district of Willemstad. Joseph's first daughter had already been born and four more children would follow. Jo gave piano, violin, singing, guitar, and mathematics lessons. He tutored children of rich families at home; whenever a student was a young lady, he gave her lessons in the presence of a chaperone.

Jo Corsen played the organ in the liberal synagogue Emanu-El and wrote music reviews. His aversion to marching music did not keep him from being bandmaster to the civic guard; after all, he had plenty of mouths to feed. He composed or wrote poetry in the evenings. "I truly live when I dream," he wrote in *Mis hijos y mis sueños*, and his dreams consisted of sounds. Some eighty-five pieces of music and one hundred of Corsen's poems have survived.

Corsen had a double talent and was the perfect man for the job of breathing life into the weekly *Notas y Letras*. Despite all this, he remained a transitional figure. Corsen struggled all his life with his great European examples. He was able to free himself of Chopin's influence, at least more so than his contemporary Paul Quirino de Lima (1861–1926), who made an adaptation for *Sé Fiel* of Chopin's Nocturne opus 9 no. 1, or his son J. M. Emirto de Lima who, under his own name, wrote the piece *Crepúsculo: Imitando música de Chopín*. At long last Corsen was able to wrench himself free from Schubert, but then Verdi came along. Ten months after the première of *Othello* in Milan, Corsen received a copy of the score—a miracle, owing to the poor travel connections of the time—and composed his *Othello Fantasie*.

"With Corsen," Wim Statius Muller told me, "there are no gimmicks; technically speaking his scores are always *tours de force*, but he only really excelled when he left behind his European models. He still didn't dare to be Antillean all the time."

It was to his merit that he at least undertook the first attempts to do so. The first section of his waltz opus no. 5 was in Viennese 3/4 time. In the second section he introduced a Spanish *pasillo* figure and, in the third section, a Venezuelan joropo figure. He sought new ways of making music and made use of the hemiola rhythm or pattern (alternating 6/8 and 3/4 time) that is so characteristic of South American dances, such as the Colombian *bambuco* and the Venezuelan joropo. After the waltz opus no. 6—which was more Iberian than the previous one—he composed three mazurka-nocturnes, and this combination alone showed just how well he knew Chopin's music: the nocturnes are not based on a dance rhythm, but Chopin could not resist giving them a hint of a mazurka.

Jo Corsen lived in a house in Pietermaai, a neighborhood built in the nineteenth century on a narrow strip of land east of Punda, between the ocean and the Waaigat, a lagoon above which the trade winds blew every morning, sometimes in excess of forty knots. It was a light blue house with three downstairs and three upstairs windows. The living quarters were upstairs, and the stairwell led to a cement patio that looked out over the ocean. In September 1877, when a hurricane raged over Curaçao and claimed the lives of some two hundred islanders, Jo Corsen descended his stairwell, witnessing the power of nature and crying out against the wind: "*Majestuoso . . . majestuoso*."

His contemporaries took him to be a romantic who had never completely lost the phlegmatic disposition of his Irish-English ancestry. He had a subtle sense of humor, loved to have a laugh, but always kept a certain amount of distance. He was Catholic, and because only a few whites on the island were, the priests constantly tried to enlist him to do work for them. They visited him several times in the hope of getting him to compose liturgical music and write devotional verse for them; he refused. He did not think it was necessary for his Protestant wife to convert to Catholicism. After they both died, this ultimately led to a definitive separation: Jo was buried in the Catholic cemetery and Féderica in the Protestant one.

Corsen was a kind, amiable man. He did not allow himself to become embroiled in the island gossip, taking part only once in a musical dispute (with Gerry Palm). He was shocked at the vehemence of his own reaction, and for the rest of his life he kept out of all the bickering envy and jockeying for position. He involved as many poets and composers in *Notas y Letras* as he could, and his sole aim was to disseminate Antillean music as much as possible.

He was, however, a perfectionist. When the weekly *La Cruz* sloppily printed one of his poems, he sent an angry letter to the editor. "Damnation," he fulminated in Papiamentu. "When you decide to include a text in your publication, pay more attention and do it with care and skill, and not like you were trying to cram some little rag into your columns at the last minute . . ." These were exactly the kind of high standards he set when editing *Notas y Letras*.

A total of seventy-two weekly issues were published. The reason it had to cease publication in 1888 had nothing to do with a lack of international interest, nor with local disinterest; the publication had an avid readership. Curaçaoans do, however, have the peculiar habit of never paying their subscription fees. The dailies and weeklies would continue to suffer from this, until they decided to collect the money in advance. The local subscribers helped kill *Notas y Letras*, which kept the island from taking the international stage.

Corsen's biographer, Fons Rutten, attributed the cause to the precarious state of the economy at the time. Tax records indicated that in 1900 only 428 of the 28,000 inhabitants had an annual income above 1,000 guilders. He forgot that the well-to-do were just as bad at defaulting as everyone else when it came to paying taxes; they disguised their real income—a practice that went on well into the twentieth century and in the time I lived there. Moreover, the merchants made the most money by selling smuggled goods from Venezuela, which they never reported to the tax authorities. For centuries Curaçao had been divided into slaves without rights and white potentates who were allowed everything. The Emancipation Decree of 1863 that freed the slaves did not have an immediate effect of rectifying this crooked situation. Well into the twentieth century the privileged class felt they were above the law and used the bills they were supposed to pay to light their barbecues. This contempt for financial obligations sounded the death knell for *Notas y Letras* and threw the music back to the confines of the island.

Corsen could not stand this. He did not become embittered, however, since it was not in his character. The name he gave to his last composition was *Many Happy Returns*, and in many other ways he expressed his gratitude to all the good life had brought him. But it still bothered him that his fellow islanders preferred their wallets to their own culture. This fact made him able to see more clearly than ever that there was something lacking in their feeling of self-worth.

In 1893 he composed a waltz that made use of the typical Dutch Antillean forms of rhythm for both the left and right hands; in 1899 he made a series of recommendations to standardize Papiamentu spelling; and in 1905 he published "Atardi," the first full-fledged poem in Papiamentu. Following the demise of *Notas y Letras* he became more intense.

His nationalism was partially the result of the total eclipse of the sun above the Andes. Jo Corsen had shared Agustín Bethencourt's ideals and had expected the sleeping giant of South America to awaken. The developments in Venezuela indicated the exact opposite; a period of chaos ensued after the liberal regime of Guzmán Blanco, and in 1905 Juan Vicente Gómez seized power in a coup. His absolute dictatorship would last for the next twenty-seven years in a climate of utter madness. Gabriel García Márquez did not make up a single word when he depicted the macabre Gómez in *The Autumn of the Patriarch*. To him people were mosquitoes: if their buzzing got in his way, they ended up as bloodstains on the wallpaper. He forbade everything a dictator could forbid, sold the petroleum rights to Shell and Standard Oil, and demanded a 10 per cent share for himself. The amount of money he received reached astronomical heights.

A period of cultural obscurity ensued that also affected Colombia, Cuba, Brazil, and Argentina. This might have been on Corsen's mind when he wrote, in "Atardi," "A night sometimes goes on for ages / how slowly it advances."

He might be able to turn his back on South America, but not on Europe. Romantic influences crept into his later work. His *Esperanza Nocturno*, which he composed shortly after the death of his uncle Chris Ulder, has such a melancholic Schubert ring to it, you almost expect the voice of Elisabeth Schwartzkopf to break out into song in German. His *Amicitia* also has a touch of Schubert—that is, for someone who first hears it in Europe.

I heard *Amicitia* in a house in Otrobanda, looked outside, and saw a black woman walking past, wearing a straw hat and carrying a bag with a watermelon in it larger than a calabash. With languidly swaying hips she entered into the evening light, and I knew that Jo Corsen must have witnessed a similar sight when he wrote down the notes—as if he wanted to render a tropical variation on the *Winterreise*.

11

The Passion for a Great-Great-Grandfather

In Curaçao the past is never far away. On every little strip of coast you can find pieces of blue glass. Water went bad in the holds of ships; mariners drank claret in the eighteenth century, light red wine poured from large blue bottles. The empty bottles were tossed into the sea, floated to the coast and broke up on the reefs. To this very day you can hear the remaining shards clinking on among the lengths of volcanic stone. I was always impressed whenever I picked up a piece of that blue glass polished by the sea. Three centuries old, I told myself: the hand of a sailor had once held this glass.

The past is just as tangible inland. Long, unbroken sections of wall from old plantations still remain intact. You do not have to look very hard to come across such a section of slave wall, and at that moment you realize how difficult the regime had been for the black population. Bloodthirsty dogs guarded those walls, so that no slave could escape.

Houses on Caribbean islands are not torn down, they rot away at the same rate as the kapok tree, which is able to withstand extended periods of drought and only slowly withers away. And when you listen to people telling stories, the past seems more a part of today than a century ago. Every day I drove past Joseph Sickman Corsen's old house in Pietermaai; pretty rundown at present, and yet easily recognizable by the shape of the windows and the stairwell to the upper floor. And I met Randal Corsen, his great-great-grandson. His full name is Randal Lucien Sickman Corsen. He too was given the middle name Sickman when he was born in 1972, along with an English name, to stress the origins of the Sickman family, and a

French one, to pay tribute to his mother's heritage. Her father had come to Curaçao from then French-speaking Lebanon.

Randal started taking piano lessons at the age of nine. At the age of eighteen he was accepted by the conservatory in Tilburg, Netherlands, after having auditioned with a work by his great-great-grandfather, Jo Corsen. He took lessons in both classical and improvised music, got his diploma, and performed several times in Curaçao. I heard him for the first time during this period. I followed his career: he formed his own trio, specialized in Latin jazz, reached the finals of the Anderson Jazz Award, won a Dutch Edison Award with his first solo CD, and started teaching at conservatories in Tilburg and Amsterdam. His career took off like a rocket.

"You're descended from Jo Corsen," his great-uncle Joseph had often told him. Or: "You're just as musical as your Aunt Yolanda." A granddaughter of Jo's, she played the violin and wrote poems under the pseudonym Oda Blinder.

As a boy Randal tried to play the pieces by his great-great-grandfather. It wasn't easy; most of them were too difficult for him. Besides, he couldn't really find a place for them in his life; at the time he preferred playing waltzes by Jacobo Palm, who composed in keys that were easier to play in, such as G major, D major, A major, or E minor. Great-great-grandfather Corsen often wrote in E♭. Later, when Randal was at the conservatory, this became his favorite key, and even later when he recorded his first CD he invariably used E♭ for the tracks. It was then that he began to wonder whether such preferences could also be biologically determined.

He used the first years of his musical career to discover his own kind of music. Randal wanted to write contemporary music, just like his great-great-grandfather had done by surveying the nineteenth-century musical idioms before setting down his first notes on paper. Jo was self-taught; he would never have been able to attend a conservatory. For him, the road to opus no. 1 was long and fraught with obstacles. Randal was able to get there sooner, though the improvisational music department at the conservatory was still in its early stages and the students often were left to their own devices.

A cousin of his was going to get married. A couple of weeks before the wedding she asked Randal to record one of Jo Corsen's waltzes for her. Again that connection to the past: she wanted to dance the first dance at the wedding reception with her father to the music of her great-great-grandfather. Looking for an appropriate waltz, Randal went through the musical scores Fons Rutten had included in his biography. That was his first foray into the music.

He started studying Jo's music in earnest and played a couple of waltzes for his classical music instructor, Frans van der Tak at the Tilburg Conservatory. Van der Tak could not believe his ears. Spanish, he thought, Albeniz; but no, not really. It was both European and South American: a delicious concoction, but not a mishmash; each and every work was well-conceived down to the last note. Randal had also come to the same conclusion; he just needed confirmation from an outsider.

In 2000 the music collector Selwyn Maduro released a CD on which a computer-guided piano played compositions by Jo Corsen. Practically no one was familiar with the works anymore. Selwyn had done missionary work, but the recording was a disappointment. Listening to the canned sound, for the first time in his life Randal felt compelled to imbue his great-great-grandfather's work with the soul of a musician.

He started looking for funding. Henry van der Kwast, chairman of the Curaçao S.E.L. Maduro Music Foundation, supplied him with the resources to hire a producer—not a Dutch one, but a Belgian.

In 1983 Wim Statius Muller recorded an LP in the Gilbert Steurbaut studio in Ghent. The Belgian was immediately charmed with Dutch Antillean music. He brought Statius Muller and the S.E.L. Maduro Music Foundation in contact with Brussels music publisher René Gailly. Starting in 1987, Gilbert Steurbaut recorded the work of at least seven Curaçaoan composers while René Gailly put the LPs and then CDs on the market. A brilliant businessman Gailly was not, but he had a client worth his weight in gold.

The Queen Elisabeth Concours rewarded all its laureates by allowing them to record an album with music of their own choice. Steurbaut made the recordings, Gailly produced them. You might say that for fifteen years the Elisabeth Concours subsidized Dutch Antillean music. In 2002 the contract terminated, and that quickly marked the end of René Gailly International Productions. From then on the S.E.L. Maduro Music Foundation produced all its own

CDs, but Gilbert Steurbaut's enthusiasm had not waned in the least and he continued making recordings in his Ghent studio.

Before Randal headed off for Ghent, he visited the Central Historical Archives in Curaçao and closely examined all of great-great-grandfather Corsen's surviving manuscripts. Some of them had been eaten away at by white ants, and on some others the titles had rotted away completely. There was a music score that abruptly ended after the second measure of the second section, but which up until then had been a detailed and meticulously notated mazurka. Randal finished the composition, completely in the style of the first part and in accordance with the musical language of his great-great-grandfather. He called it a "restoration."

In total he selected twenty-three pieces for the CD; that was all the single disc could hold. If it were up to him, he would have recorded every single work; there was not one he thought was below par.

Family pride? He was afraid so. He played the pieces for Wim Statius Muller and Robert Rojer. "Not what I expected," said Rojer. Of all the nineteenth-century composers, Corsen was the one who had faded the most into the background. Randal gradually discovered why that was so. Keeping in mind what the consumers of musical scores wanted, Curaçaoan composers did not want to make it too difficult for amateurs to play, so they avoided the black keys. Not too many sharps, not too many flats. Corsen used them in abundance. And then there was something else: after the disastrous downfall of *Notas y Letras*, hardly any of his new musical scores appeared in print. He no longer took into account what amateurs wanted, but composed solely what he could perform himself. Corsen was a gifted pianist who had little difficulty playing even the most virtuoso works by Gottschalk. For the same reason—the fact that no one bought his scores anymore—toward the end of his life he bid farewell to dance music and concentrated on composing serious music.

He had reached the highest possible level for someone with no formal training. "You have to see him in his regional context," in Randal's opinion. "And then you can conclude he was in no way inferior to Gottschalk or the Cuban Cervantes. He had his own style, he is original. You can tell by his music that he is a poet; he pays a great deal of attention to the melody, he lets them sing in an Iberian way. His compositions are well thought out, he makes frequent use of polyrhythm, is technically quite proficient. None of his scores lack a single piece of performance or dynamic notation. There is something fanatical about his way of writing, as though he had to do his very best since he was self-taught. And sometimes he is surprisingly modern. He uses the augmented fourth, which today is frequently used in jazz."

Jo Corsen has become a passion for Randal Corsen. "If someone were to ask me about typical Dutch Antillean classical music, I would let them hear Corsen, not Blasini or Jan Gerard Palm. Other composers tend more toward the folkloric; Jo showed the way to the future. Had he lived another twenty years—he was fifty-eight when he died—I think he would have succeeded in mixing jazz with Antillean music."

In his waltz *Simpatia,* he added a syncopated bass to the accompaniment that, in the second section, he brings to the fore. In the second section the rhythm is reminiscent of *tambú* and *tumba,* and is straight out of Africa. Unbelievable, thinks his great-great-grandson: "so modern, that's what I do today, only now it's called Latin jazz."

12

A Wrong Modulation

In 1871 the Jewish businessman Jacob J. Naar had a theatre built in the Pietermaai district of Willemstad. It was an elegant building in classical style, with tall substructure under an arched roof. Although it was not huge, it was distinguished, because of its six pillars, the Doric portico in three sections, the three pilasters against the façade, the frieze in a cornice, and especially because of its monumental double spiral staircase. Its ochre colored walls were in sharp contrast to the clouds blown by the trade winds above the mirroring waters; the back of the theatre faced the sea.

The hurricane of 1877 blew off the roof and tidal waves washed away the seats. Not bothered by a shadow of a doubt, Jacob Naar undertook the task of restoration. Ever since, the building has withstood all storms. The government took over the building in the 1930s and gave it another function, but only renovated the interior. You can still climb its majestic staircase and run your hand over the brazilwood (pernambuco) railing. At the time this was the best place for a rendezvous with a young lady—during intermission, visitors hurried outside to catch a sigh of sea breeze, and on the staircase there were no chaperones.

Jacob Naar was a music fanatic. He taught his own son Emilio to become a violinist; he brought opera companies to Curaçao, as well as Spanish, Mexican, and Venezuelan *zarzuela* groups and violinists, cellists, and pianists from Cuba, Mexico, Haiti, Venezuela, Portugal, and France. The opera companies consisted solely of singers. To accompany them, Naar enlisted the services of such pianists as Jules Blasini, Chris Ulder, Jo Corsen, Jan Gerard Palm, and in the twentieth century, Rudolf or Jacobo Palm. They often had to play Donizetti, Bellini, Rossini, or Verdi, and something of these composers' styles began to permeate their own compositions. Under the influence of Italian opera, the Curaçaoan waltzes and dances became increasingly melodious.

The theatre also housed the recently formed symphony orchestra. Theater Naar lasted fifty years; when it closed the symphony orchestra was quickly disbanded. The island turned out to be too small after all for a genuine symphony orchestra.

For Rudolf Boskaljon, the dissolving of the orchestra was proof that "musical life never blossomed in Curaçao." Rudolf (1887–1970) was the son of bandmaster Johannes Boskaljon (1863–1936). Johannes, nicknamed Janchi, played flute, tenor horn, and practically every other wind instrument; Rudolf played violin and cello. It was perfectly understandable why they of all people were disappointed when the symphony orchestra disbanded. In the twentieth century Rudolf made a second attempt at forming and maintaining a symphony orchestra. Under his leadership the Curaçao Symphony Orchestra lasted five years. Even after that, he never said die, and in 1939 he tried for a third time. This time he achieved success with the Curaçao Philharmonic Orchestra, which would survive to celebrate its fifth anniversary. Most of its members were amateurs, who often had to be supplemented by musicians from Caracas, and in the end it died a quiet death, two years before the passing of its founder.

In 1958, Rudolf was commissioned to write the history of the first century of Dutch Antillean musical life. The book was written in a minor key. Boskaljon tried to elevate the local music scene to that of Europe and, just like Sisyphus, he watched the boulder continually roll back down the hill. He did the best he could, took the boat to the Netherlands, studied that country's music education programs, and, when he returned, he founded his music school. When Theater Naar ceased to exist he took the initiative to have the Municipal Theatre built. When the Nazis came to power and Jewish artists had to flee Europe, he invited Isaac Stern, Yasha Heifetz, Yehudi Menuhin, and Arthur Rubinstein. He twice brought Lili Kraus to the island and twice organized a performance by Claudio Arrau. All to his credit, the only thing he regretted time after time was not being able to allow them to play a violin or piano concerto, for lack of a decent orchestra. For Boskaljon, the measures of all music were Brahms and Beethoven.

Grandiose, serious, and majestic were unsuitable adjectives to describe the Caribbean way of life. You might say, how fortunate. Symphony orchestra culture was always subject to fits and starts and never really matured; this relieved the local composers of having to compose symphonic works. At the end of the nineteenth century the general consensus was that they ought to limit themselves to smaller pieces, to chamber music that could be performed by a solo piano, pieces for piano and violin, or for a small ensemble. This observation had a liberating rather than limiting effect. Local composers no longer had to measure up to what was going on in Vienna, Berlin, or Amsterdam; they could go their own way.

In practically every home you could hear mazurkas, waltzes, and other dances played on the piano, violin, or guitar, and in the smaller houses on the four-stringed *cuarta* (*cuatro*)—the poor man's guitar. The military brass band played twice a week on the square in Otrobanda. Warships and passenger liners alike were welcomed by the same brass band playing Curaçao waltzes when they entered the harbor.

Local music flourished—the kind that began to distinguish itself more and more from European music. Boskaljon thought this was nice, in the way that the drawing of a child can be considered to have some artistic merit, though no more than that. For him, you had real music—the European kind—and bad music, the local music, the *muzik di zumbi*, the music of the spirits, or the mangled dance rhythms the blacks played. "The one who plays the melody," he scoffed, "is usually a flutist, who has never had a single day of musical instruction in his life, but who buys a cheap instrument with five or six keys, who (except for the octave key) ties them together with twine, because they get in his way, and who attempts to wheedle some kind of waltz or *danza* out of the instrument."

He was not conservative; he asked foreign soloists to play Bartók and Stravinsky, De Falla and Albeniz, Debussy and Ravel. Nor was he a racist; one of the musicians he encouraged the most was the black guitarist and double bass player Julián Coco from the working-class neighborhood Colón. At the end of the 1930s, he brought an American baritone over to sing Negro spirituals. But on his island, he rejected the African influences. "One should most certainly not attempt to ascribe any religious rituals or magical attributes to the music."

He received support in his efforts to propagate European music by local composer Carl Fensohn. His name only appears as a footnote in books, but back then Fensohn was in practically every review that appeared. Fensohn was born in Hamburg in 1850 and settled in Curaçao in 1878. As a businessman he was declared bankrupt several times, but in the Curaçao String Quartet, the Curaçao Symphonic Orchestra, and soon in the entire Curaçaoan music scene, he played first violin. By the name they gave him, Don Carlos, you would not have thought he attached much significance to his origins, but together with Boskaljon he was a fervent advocate of German music.

The two gentlemen did not think much of Chopin, let alone Antillean mazurkas. When the Shell Oil refinery opened, the wind was in their sails. Within half a century the population grew from thirty thousand to one hundred thousand and the number of Dutchmen increased by the thousands. At Shell's expense, quite a few Dutch musicians took the boat to Curaçao; and after a performance in the Municipal Theatre, they played in Club Asiento, the society club set up for the Shell cadre. In the 1920s it looked as though European music would prevail, with German music at the forefront.

Then, on the other side of the ocean, the political climate changed. After Hitler came to power, the Honorary Counsel on Curaçao resigned from office. Carl Fensohn represented Austria on the island and, out of a sense of duty, he represented the interests of German nationals on Curaçao. In 1938 came the *Anschluss* with Austria, and from that moment on Fensohn was seen to represent both Austria and Germany. On the day that Germany invaded the Netherlands, he was declared an enemy of the state on the grounds of his nationality and was arrested and transported to an internment camp on Bonaire. The same fate befell his daughter Adelaide, members of the NSB (the Dutch National Socialist party), German sailors who happened to be on ships that were anchored in port at the time, and Jewish refugees with a German or Austrian passport. Fensohn spent a year and a half behind barbed wire; no one wanted to have anything to do with him when he returned to Curaçao. He passed away in 1942. Four men carried him to his grave: the three remaining members of the Curaçao String Quartet and the timpanist from the Curaçao Philharmonic Orchestra.

Curaçaoan musicians had to struggle much longer against European influences than did their counterparts in Cuba, Martinique, Guadeloupe, Puerto Rico, and Santo Domingo. And as with every struggle, they did not always take a united stand.

Immediately following the emergence of their own music, the musicians started attacking one another. The slightest pretense was enough; in 1867 a polemic arose in *De Curaçaosche Courant* about a single wrong modulation in a work by Jan Gerard Palm. Every colleague entered the fray. Jan Gerard—Gerry—experimented with dissonance and tended toward the atonal. According to Chris Ulder, he went too far on that one occasion. Gerry defended himself and Jo Corsen took Chris Ulder's side, after which Jules Blasini defended Gerry. The music teachers Van Dinter and Quast tried to calm down the composers, but despite their soothing words they continued to pour scorn on one another.

Around the turn of the century, Jacobo Conrad (1879–1918) took up the challenge. He does not appear at all in Boskaljon's music history; at first he had problems reading music, later with writing it, and yes, Boskaljon did indeed consider people like him to be illiterates. Jacobo Conrad was a tragic figure: too much rum, too many women, and too much animosity. He was at loggerheads with practically everybody. You could not tell by looking at him; on the two surviving photographs he looks like some fragile yet extremely strict schoolteacher with a monocle ensconced on his right eye and a white bowtie under his brown, almost black chin. He was a romantic through and through, serenading the women he courted every evening with the violin under his chin he had excelled at playing ever since childhood. He moved people, but his tendency of pursuing married women always got him into trouble. On top of everything, he suffered from midget-like proportions and he hid his insecurity behind strongly held opinions. There was no such thing as a quiet conversation with him at his home in Otrobanda; he would soon leap out of his chair, raise his voice, and make heated gestures. He was a know-it-all with strong views when it came to music.

"He was not much taller than I was when I was eleven," Edgar Palm recalls. As a child he was often tormented because of it. Yet he was a natural talent and was allowed to play with older musicians, who often regarded him as some kind of circus attraction, putting him on a table to play behind the orchestra. He never missed a party; he was cheered, especially since he was so touching—a tiny little squirt with such a big violin on his shoulder. He summoned up his courage by drinking heavily.

His real name was Elias Martinus. The name revealed quite a lot; for Jacobo, perhaps much too much. Elias points to a Jewish father, Martinus a black mother. He was raised by Leopold Ibarra, who sent him to elementary school and made him take extra Spanish lessons. Ibarra came from a Venezuelan family. He also gave him a violin, which the little dark boy did not want to let go of, even when he had to go to bed: he slept with the instrument next to his pillow. Elias took a pseudonym—Jacobo Conrad—and let himself be called Coco Lepol. Lepol was his foster father's nickname.

Coco Lepol married a gorgeous, dignified dark woman, but could not give up flirting. Chenda overlooked quite a few of his transgressions and saved many of his compositions by locking them in a cabinet, which she guarded like a lioness. Once he had finished a waltz or some other dance piece, Coco Lepol never paid any more attention to it, hurrying into town for another of his nocturnal serenades or visiting a friend who owned a grocery and liquor store. Whenever anyone came looking for him at home, Chenda would say, "You can find him in Keukenstraat," for that's where the liquor store was located.

His loveliest waltzes—*Pan Angelical* and *10 de Junio*—were written for Chenda, who had been born on the tenth of June. They did not earn him much money; all the same, he refused to get a job. Coco Lepol lived for his music.

He modeled the waltz after the danza and expanded it into three sections. He always concluded the first section with a long *fermata,* doing the same with the second section. In the final section he recapitulated the harmonic line of the first section. The first and final sections could often be fast, while the middle section was slow, or vice versa. He transformed the European waltz into an Antillean one, with three parts and just as melodious as a danza.

He went a step further than Corsen had in looking more intensively for a more Caribbean sense of individuality. To him, musical notes had to jump like sparks, waltzes had to crackle like fire—after all, life was a fleeting, incandescent flame.

He died at the age of thirty-nine of a liver disorder. But he passed on his ideas to the Palm family, who for the entire twentieth century would be the pivotal figures of Dutch Antillean music.

13

The Palms

I was able to put a few questions to the last Palm before he lost his memory. Of all the performances he gave, Edgar especially remembers the 1962 opening of the FIDE Candidates Tournament, to which he had added luster. As is often the case with openings, no one was listening to the music, except for one chess player, a tall, thin young man who sat listening as if mesmerized. "Your music fills me with total serenity," he said after the performance. The otherwise modest Edgar Palm was flattered; the chess player who shook his hand was Bobby Fischer.

Edgar Palm gave his final performance in 1996, two years before his death at the age of ninety-three. During his farewell concert he designated Norman Morón as his successor, and the entire hall gasped with astonishment: it was not to be a Palm. From then on Curaçao would never be the same island. A Palm had played on each and every memorable occasion. For the very last time Edgar began playing the first strains of the waltz *Maria Cecilia*, and for the last time the Curaçaoans swayed to its lilting phrases. That marked the end of an era that lasted longer than most royal houses.

The musical dynasty began with Jan Gerard Palm. He belonged to the fifth generation that had settled in the Dutch Antilles. The first Palm, who left from the Swedish port of Karlskona with the Christian name of Hermanus, embarked on a West India Company ship that crossed the Atlantic and landed at Curaçao. Eight of the ten men who signed off in the colony were crewmen (for those journeying as passengers could consider themselves lucky indeed to receive any food or drink while on board); seven of them were not Dutch nationals.

To man its ships, the West India Company recruited seafarers from Sweden, Norway, Denmark, northern Germany, Poland, and the Baltic countries. The oldest colonists on Curaçao bore such names as Druschky, Eskilden, and Faarup. The Druschky, Hoyer, and Weeber families came from Polish Silesia—probably another reason why the mazurka was such a hit in the Antilles.

Hermanus Palm was not even eighteen at the time he headed for the West Indies, but he was already a widower. That may perhaps explain his wish to cross the ocean and begin a new life. On Curaçao he wasted no time and married for the second time at the age of nineteen. He set sail again at age twenty, this time as boatswain on the schooner *Buena Fortuna*.

He may have been related to the Swedish composer Johan Frederik Palm, an organist who wrote several religious hymns. At any rate, Hermanus was able to read music and from time to time he slid behind the keys of the church organ and played music together with his children.

His son Johannes became Curaçao's first music teacher. You might even call him a forerunner. After Johannes, things went quiet for three generations. Then everything exploded: in the end no fewer than eighteen Palms went on to do something related to music—either as piano tuner, pianist, organist, bass player, clarinetist in a dance orchestra, professional musician, or, as it was so quaintly called in the Curaçao civil registry, as Master of Music.

Jan Gerard (1831–1906) was the first composer in the Palm family. His long, white beard made him look quite the patriarch. Just like Johann Sebastian Bach, he involved his entire family in music. He gave music lessons to his sons Cornelis and George Mount, his niece Betsy, his grandson Jacobo, and his nephews John and Rudolf. Jacobo, Rudolf, and John would all become composers. Rudolf was father to the composers Albert and Edgar, and Jacobo to the violinist Irma Cecilia. Since the same names kept cropping up in the various musical branches, it is quite confusing, even for the descendants. Edgar, for instance, who wrote a reference book on Antillean music, kept mixing up two Jan Gerards. On top of that, they all had nicknames: Jan Gerard was called Shon Gerry—the Papiamentu word *shon* derives from *señor* or seigneur and was turned into an honorary title given to a man or woman worthy of respect—Rudolf, Shon Dòdò; Jacobo, Shon Coco. But there was no mistaking one thing: the name Palm is synonymous with Dutch Antillean dance music.

They were just as strict with themselves as they were with their pupils. Quite a few Palms were born in the Ijzerstraat (Iron Street), and the children were given a spartan upbringing. Jan Gerard never gave a piano lesson without a ruler at hand and he was known for being capable of mercilessly whacking his pupil's fingers. When it came to duty and a sense of order, the Palms remained Swedish Protestants. But under the Caribbean sun their disposition turned flamboyant and they were intoxicated with women and parties.

A Palm was someone who laughed, and the only form of gloominess they succumbed to was melancholia. The only Palm who exhibited serious symptoms of this was the highly gifted Tonie Palm, whose full name was Jean Bernard Antonie Palm. His life was like a novella: he refused to play a single note after the death of his mother. Born in 1885, he turned his back on music in 1905. By then he had composed six *danzas* in the style of the Puerto Rican master Juan Morel Campos, five waltzes, the mazurka *El desengaño*, and the melody to the Antillean national anthem. Tonie would live to be fifty-nine years old, but without any more music.

The Palms were courteous, in a most refined way. Every late afternoon, Jacobo Palm took a walk with his father through Otrobanda. They always avoided going down a certain street. When Jacobo asked why, his father told him that he had lent some money to someone who lived on that street. By walking past his house, it would be a painful reminder to him that he still owed him and that might damage his honor and reputation.

A Palm played more than one instrument, following the example of Jan Gerard, who was just as fanatic playing piano as he was playing organ, lute, clarinet, flute, and mandolin. Shon Dòdò (1880–1950) gave piano or organ lessons in the morning, and in late afternoon guitar, *cuarta*, mandolin, or banjo lessons, and evenings he played double bass, saxophone, or clarinet in a dance band. He was also the player-piano specialist on the island and the one who repaired *Ka'i-orgels*, small, square barrel organs that were imported from Italy via Venezuela and used at smaller parties and functions, in place of a dance band.

A Palm sacrificed everything for the sake of music, if need be, even himself. John Palm (1885–1925) lent his clarinet to anyone and everyone who wanted to play it, and had to pay for it with his life: he became fatally infected by tuberculosis.

As a young boy John had been a rascal, but compared to his cousin Ra he was an angel. Ra had the habit of randomly snatching babies away from their mothers. He used to climb up on a roof, dance with the baby across the roofing tiles, and sometimes toss it in the air. The mothers screamed at him from the street. "Ra, give me back my baby. Ra, stop being so mean."

Once they had become adults, the Palms changed into dutiful pillars of society. They composed music behind a writing desk, never behind a piano keyboard. For Shon Dòdò it was truly a ritual: on his square working table he had a pot with red and a pot with blue ink, sheets of music notation paper, a slate pencil, and an ample supply of fountain pens, rubber erasers, and blotting paper. Straight across from him was a bottle of glue. Whenever he decided to change large sections, he glued a piece of manuscript paper over the previous one and rewrote the passage. Every evening after dinner he slid behind his working table and worked until late at night. For the Palms all had one thing in common: they did not want to be outdone by Jan Gerard, the patriarch who had more than a hundred works to his name.

A younger Palm played the music of an elder Palm to keep the music of the clan alive. The Palms looked after their own and gave each other work; they formed ensembles in which other Palms especially could shine. In the small musical world they invariably picked out the sunny spots and overshadowed their contemporaries. As a composer, Joseph Sickman Corsen was in no way inferior to Jan Gerard, but he could not avail himself of a gang of nephews and nieces able to perform his works at each and every party or festive occasion.

The Palms knew the score when it came to the Caribbean music world, and whoever dared to cast doubt on their compositional talents could count on being reprimanded. It happened to Chris Ulder, and he was so angry he once sent a stinging letter to the editor about it, inveighing:

> Jan Gerard Palm, he who sets the tone and can never be praised enough, the exalted world famous composer has reprimanded me.

> That reprimand was more than deserved, for I, novice dilettante that I am, ought not to have deigned to judge the work of the grand Master, let alone suggest a way of improving it. The man, who is at home in every conceivable musical genre, who composes in his sleep; the man who, when devotional music is involved, overshadows Bach, Mozart, Händel, Rossini and Van Bree; the man, whose profundity surpasses a Mendelssohn Bartholdy, a Beethoven in instrumentation, in melody, a Bellini; the man whose artistic body of work far outdistances Weber, Auber, Boieldeu, Meyerbeer, Halevy, Donizetti, Verdi, and Flotow; the man whose music in terms of sheer imaginative force triumphs over Wagner, the friend of the Bavarian king . . . , may indeed be indignant at the audacity of a novice. . . . Forgive me, I beseech Thee, O Bavarian Genius, Goliathic Composer, *Jungfrausche* Poet, forgive me, O PALM of Palms . . .

The reference Ulder makes to him being able to compose in his sleep has to do with *Canto de los Angeles*, one of Jan Gerard Palm's most famous pieces. The waltz owed its existence to a dream in which singing angels took Gerry away. The second section is one bar too long; the normal length was either sixteen or thirty-two bars, but the Canto contained thirty-three bars, seventeen plus sixteen. Shon Gerry loved to tell the story that it was impossible to get rid of a bar of music that had been revealed to him by angels. He had solved the problem by letting a *fermata*, or long pause, follow the seventeenth bar.

That he suffered from a certain degree of mythomania cannot be denied. He held his head high and not just for musical reasons. Small islands are big prisons (Boeli van Leeuwen); colonies were also breeding grounds for conformity. If you did not respond to slander or malicious gossip with fortitude and an indomitable look in your eyes, you were lost or turned into a wreck in no time. No one held it against Gerry that he had been with a dark woman when he was a young man—that was a matter of course among white men—but the fact he had openly admitted it created bad blood.

She was not black, as I would hear over and over again on Curaçao, also from the mouths of his great-great-grandchildren; Maria Simona was a full-blooded Indian. Her relationship with Jan Gerard had not lasted long. She had only spent one full night with him. A quarter of a century later Jan Gerard acknowledged his son Antonio

Manuel at the Court of Justice and gave him his last name. For mid-nineteenth-century standards, the former was more or less customary; the latter was so exceptional that many an upstanding citizen took it as a provocation.

His late-nineteenth-century namesake Jan Gerard did the same; he recognized his son John and even went one step further: at the age of nineteen he married the Indian woman Maria Viras, with whom he had had a relationship since he was sixteen. To top it all off, he had her name changed at the Court of Justice, to Maria Felice Celestina—Heavenly Blissful Maria—to make clear to the public at large that he did not consider it a scandal in the least to have taken the kitchen maid in his arms at the age of sixteen.

Like a great many white families in the nineteenth century, the Palms became Antilleanized. In 1850 the number of free coloreds outnumbered the number of slaves on Curaçao: eight thousand as opposed to two thousand seven hundred. Mulattoes often led prosperous lives. Jewish fathers had their bastard sons learn a trade and bought them a store or a workplace. Colored shopkeepers often earned more than the working-class white Protestants.

Being white did not automatically mean you were more influential or prosperous. Conversely, black was synonymous with being poor and without rights. In the Dutch colonies the Emancipation Law abolishing slavery was instituted only in 1863, thirty years after the abolition of slavery in the English colonies and fifteen years after the French. During the final years of slavery, half the population of Curaçao felt they were heavily discriminated against by the other half, also since the black inhabitants of Haiti, Jamaica, Trinidad, Puerto Rico, Martinique, and Guadeloupe had already been living in freedom for quite some time. The abolition of slavery had taken much too long, and when the Netherlands finally bowed to international pressure, it took another thirty years before the blacks left the plantations, for the simple reason that the freed slaves had no other place to go to make a living. In their yards they wove Panama hats, in 1902 alone one and a half million of them. For the black population, actual emancipation began in 1915 when Shell began constructing the oil refinery and Catholic priests from the Dutch province of Brabant began tackling illiteracy and setting up schools all over the island.

Coloreds were much better off; they could read and write, had professions, and had the same rights under the law as whites. Still, quite a few of them felt like second-class citizens. They did not quite belong either to the whites or to the blacks, the latter regarding them as sycophants. The poet Nydia Ecury told me that in 1942 she had been hired by the Lago Refinery on Aruba, which was part of the Standard Oil concern. Her father, who ran a Ford car dealership, had enough money to send her and her brothers and sisters to an advanced elementary school. Nydia began her job at the rank of clerk first class. Her mastery of English allowed her to rise to the position of translator, proofreader, and journalist for the *Aruba Esso News*. For eight years she worked on the first floor of the office building with the white "foreign staff," but if she wanted to use the bathroom she had to go downstairs to the restrooms for the "locally hired," for coloreds and blacks.

It is hard to tell whether or not they were troubled by discrimination because of the color of their skin. After his affair with the Indian woman, Jan Gerard married a Curaçaoan woman of Scottish descent, with whom he fathered four children, so most of the Palm children were not colored. Yet the descendants of later generations who were colored were no less well off in social terms than whites.

When I suggested that for coloreds composing meant more than just writing music, that it was a way to earn a reputation for oneself and entrance into white society, the reaction I got from composer Robert Rojer (a grandson of Jacobo Palm) was this was a "white way of thinking" and, besides, not true at all. I sincerely thought it was, and the pianist Johnny Kleinmoedig, a pupil of Edgar Palm's, supported me in this—yes, music offered the opportunity for rapid emancipation and that is why it was so practiced so fanatically. But Robert Rojer was adamant: colored musicians did not mope around acting pitiful. On the contrary, they tended to be arrogant. They felt they were rhythmically superior to the whites, and melodically superior to the blacks. To top it all off, they considered themselves to be more romantic and sensual. Jacobo, John, Alberto, and Edgar Palm, who were all slightly colored, were held in high regard as citizens, as full members of the Antillean community, and as musicians, teachers, and composers.

Toward the end of the nineteenth century the Palms were allowed to become Freemasons. You had to be high on the rungs of the social ladder to be considered for candidate membership; the lodge was choosy, on Curaçao as well, but being brown or light brown was not an obstacle: Rudolf, John, Alberto, and Edgar were all accepted as members on the basis of their artistic achievements.

This afforded them, as well as all the other musicians and composers on Curaçao, an additional benefit. To start with, in the Masonic Lodge at the Rif in Otrobanda, there was an ancient German piano, an Adams, and Edgar Palm always brought his tuning fork with him when he attended a meeting during which Masonic hymns were sung. But later on they put in a top-quality Pleyel grand piano.

"Crystal and water," Chopin had said about the Pleyel brand. "A silvery, slightly muffled sound. A light touch." Chopin had no less than three Pleyels in his Parisian apartment. Willemstad was not so well endowed. There was no shortage of pianos; when the authorities introduced a property tax in 1908, "the ownership of pianos" was regarded as the second grounds for the tax. But a Pleyel concert grand piano was in a league all by itself, and the only one was in the lodge.

Freemasons acknowledge the existence of a Supreme Being, without believing in a specific God. They are not total atheists, but when it comes to matters of faith, they keep their options open. That too proved to work in the Palms' favor; as Freemasons they were allowed to play the organs in the Protestant churches, the Catholic churches, and both Jewish synagogues. After all, they had to earn their daily *funchi*, corn bread.

The Palms were organists, bandmasters for the civil militia, conductors or first violinists in the symphony orchestra, and leaders of the dance bands that played at weddings, parties, and social functions. They composed for several different instruments, including the Ka'i-orgel (barrel organ).

And they gave music lessons.

14

Your Tempi!

For a very long time Curaçao was very Jewish. Without the substantial Sephardic Jewish community, its music could never have rivalled that of Cuba and Puerto Rico. From the seventeenth century onward, Jewish families were the ones who defined the social atmosphere and mentality of the island.

In 1732 Mikvé-Israël-Emmanuel was consecrated, the first synagogue in the Western hemisphere. As a visual symbol of Jewish integration, the egg-yellow building with three clock gables was inside the city walls of Punda, the oldest district on the island. From the very first day of their arrival, the Sephardic Jews were allowed to address the local government authorities in their own language, namely, in standard Portuguese. In 1824 they received full citizens' rights; before that, colonial civil servants had turned a blind eye when it came to them being able to purchase land, buildings, or houses.

After a schism in the latter of part of the 1870s, a second synagogue emerged. The building, belonging to the liberal Jewish community, looks more like a church. Because of where it is situated, right on the ocean, the frail towers of the Temple Emanu-El dominate the Willemstad skyline.

In both of the synagogues together, some fourteen hundred Jews attended services. In the eighteenth century their numbers were considerably more substantial: two thousand, outnumbering the white Protestants. In economically difficult times, the island offered too few employment opportunities to well-educated young men, who emigrated to Venezuela, Panama, or the United States. However, the core of the Curaçaoan middle class remained Jewish and until well into the twentieth century they owned thirty percent of all land and buildings.

The Palms gave violin and piano lessons to Jewish young ladies. All they had to do was go down the single long street that stretched for kilometers through the Scharloo district, where practically all the Jews lived, in houses so baroque they looked like they had been coated in marzipan.

One late afternoon in the nineteen twenties, Rudolf Palm was making his way home. Shon Dòdò had again just finished giving seven or eight lessons, and as usual he had bellowed his comments to the Jewish girls through the opened shutters, who were diligently applying themselves to their study of the piano. "Not so hard," he cried, "*piano, piano*" or "*rubato, rubato*."

He heard the sound of a polonaise coming from one of the houses. "Pay attention to the *tempi*," Shon Dòdò called out in Papiamentu. A dishevelled head of hair thrust out the window. "What the hell are you crying about?" "Your tempi," Shon Dòdò repeated. "May I know who you are?" Shon Dòdò went inside to introduce himself. And the man said, "Well, nice to meet you. Arthur Rubinstein."

The already famous Rubinstein had interrupted his sea voyage to be a guest for a week with a Jewish family in Scharloo. He would have been on his way to Buenos Aires or Santiago de Chile, where after World War I he had continued the international success that had begun with his performances in Spain.

Rubinstein soon paid the Palms a visit. He went to Rudolf, the outgoing one, the *bon vivant*, whose name until the age of twenty-five had been Higinio Teodosia and who was not very attached to the change of name which the Court of Justice had granted in 1905, after his father had recognized him as his son: even then everybody called him Dòdò. But he also visited the much more formal Jacobo, who, however politely and shyly, criticized the maestro's *toucher*. Too heavy-handed, he thought.

Rubinstein was not angry in the least, taking it all in with a smile—a puzzling reaction for anyone who has read his two-volume autobiography. Rubinstein had been admired his entire life by thousands upon thousands of adoring fans, but, most of all, the admiration had come from himself. Maybe he was taken by surprise by the criticism levelled at him, as some peculiar utterance he had never heard with his own ears before; or perhaps he thought of Jacobo in the first place as a composer and not as a rival pianist.

Rubinstein was not only a gifted interpreter of Chopin; he was also extremely fond of Spanish music. One of his most beautiful recordings is of Manuel de Falla's *Nuits dans les jardins d'Espagne.* In the compositions by the family Palm, Rubinstein heard the same lilting melodies reminiscent of Iberian music.

There is an anecdote about Rubinstein doing the rounds on Curaçao. As a boy, Arthur had been quite bashful. He would later turn into a glutton for erotic love, but when he got engaged, he was still unfamiliar with the proper finger positions of making love. Shon Dòdò, born in 1880 and seven years older than Rubinstein, knew as a true-born Curaçaoan what to do with Arthur's lack of experience. He referred him to one of Otrobanda's shadier hotels, and to a somewhat motherly type of lady. Rubinstein left the hotel room on cloud nine and immediately wanted to telegraph his fiancé in New York about the progress he had made down the amorous paths of love. Shon Dòdò dissuaded him from making this mistake. "You know," he told him, "if everything works out she'll notice by herself. And if she doesn't notice, then you ought to come back some time."

I doubt whether there is any truth to this story. In his autobiography, Arthur Rubinstein has a high opinion of his own libido. The mother of his friend Frederic Harman was unable to resist the charms of the seventeen-year-old pianist and kissed him passionately. He had already had an affair with his landlady Mrs. Winter when he was a student living in Berlin—at age fourteen. In Paris he had been taken to a hotel by a dancer from the Folies Bergères, who immediately solicited her mother's help to satisfy the young Pole. The only implausibility to this story was the fact that both ladies had asked for payment afterwards.

In that same Paris, during the premiere of Richard Strauss's *Salomé,* he had angered the soprano Emma Destinn, and indeed he had behaved rather clumsily, as he would write with great humor three quarters of a century later in his autobiography. He sat next to her during the supper and held forth in order to impress the leading lady of Salomé. "The way you sing is a good lesson for me. You let me hear the right way to use rubato. From now on I shall try to emulate your perfect breathing technique in my own way of phrasing, and I am certain that this is precisely what Chopin had in mind at those moments when he indicated rubato in the musical score."

Emma Destinn listened with flagging attention. All of a sudden she grabbed her champagne glass and threw it against the open hearth, shouting: "Oh yes, oh yes, I know that I'm a good singer. But I'm also a woman."

Rubinstein was no longer a young man when he travelled to South America for the first time in 1917; he celebrated his thirtieth birthday in Buenos Aires. It is also true that he did not marry until he was forty. Curaçao is not mentioned at all in the two volumes of his autobiography, even though it is perfectly possible he wanted to keep silent about that part of his life. Biographies are quite often inaccurate, just as often as are some juicy anecdotes, for that matter.

I could not find out which Jewish family had put Rubinstein up during his stay. However, May Henríquez-Alvares Correa did confirm that she had once had the honor of shaking the renowned pianist's hand in Scharloo and that he had listened attentively to the Antillean dances the Palms had performed.

So Rubinstein had become acquainted with the local music. And no one had asked him what he thought about the Caribbean mazurkas. It is a huge blunder that cannot be made good. Rubinstein had grown up in Lodz and Warsaw. When someone had told him that the pianist Josef Lhévinne was an exceptionally good interpreter of Chopin's mazurkas, Chopin was adamant in his denial: "That's quite impossible. Mr. Lhévinne cannot play mazurkas. He is a Russian!"

Curaçao and Poland have in common that they have practically always been occupied by foreign powers and, in the absence of their own sovereign ruler, they have designated the piano as their king. Rubinstein (1887–1982) had been heavily influenced by Ignaz Friedman (1882–1948), and Friedman in turn had taken lessons from Theodor Leschetizky (1830–1915). Most Poles agreed that no pianist could play mazurkas better than Friedman. Friedman himself explained that was because of his childhood in the country: at the age of six he had started dancing the mazurka at village festivities and the rhythm had lodged firmly not just in his fingers but in his legs as well. He recorded twelve mazurkas in 1929 and 1930, which the classical Naxos label reissued at the end of the twentieth century in the series *Great Pianists*. Friedman's secret was that he hesitated for a fraction of a second before attacking the third beat of the mazurka and that sometimes the rhythmic left hand part sounded much louder than the right hand. European musicologists regard that way of playing to be inimitable, but then they had never listened to Curaçaoan pianists who play exactly the same way.

Rubinstein must have noticed that. There in Scharloo, he must have cupped his hand to his ear and shook his head in disbelief. On a miniscule island on the other side of the ocean he had once again heard the essence of the Polish mazurka. Unfortunately, no one registered his amazement.

Rubinstein returned to Curaçao in 1939 to give a performance. On December 11, he quite appropriately played *Evocación* from Albeniz's *Iberian Suite* and four works by Chopin. His encore was a mazurka.

After the concert he was a guest at Chris Engels and Lucilia Engels-Boskaljon's gorgeously restored stately home Stroomzigt, with its ocean view at Rif near Otrobanda. Someone slid behind the piano and started playing a Curaçaoan waltz in such an infectious way that Rubinstein asked Dr. Engel's mother-in-law to dance, the still very attractive Mrs. Boskaljon. "My knees are shot to hell," she said. "Oh," Rubinstein replied, "so are mine."

Nearly forty years later he told this story to Wim Statius Muller, who just happened to be dining at an adjacent table in a restaurant in Rome. Despite his advanced years, for Statius Muller, Rubinstein was still the undisputed master interpreter of Chopin's works and he could not refrain from shaking the living legend's hand.

"Curaçao, 1939 . . ."

Rubinstein narrowed his eyes slightly.

"One of those fast, lively waltzes by one of the Palms. And the wonderful thing about it was it was being played by a ten-year-old boy . . ."

"You're right," said Wim, "that was me."

15

Every Child Brings Its Own Bread

Jacobo Palm, who accused Rubinstein of having a heavy touch, was a handsome man. One meter seventy-six tall, never more than sixty-three kilos. Athletic build, wiry. He no doubt owed his striking facial features to his paternal grandmother, the full-blooded Indian.

"It was never hard for me," his grandson Robert Rojer told me, "to imagine that proud hooked nose of his that defined his profile had descended from Winnetou, the Indian chief in Karl May* stories. At the same token he could very well have passed for a Spaniard. In old pictures he has the macho look of a matador. But in person he radiated peace and grace."

He was vain when it came to his body and he was always formally dressed in a suit and tie. No one ever caught him in shirtsleeves outside the house; he always wore a Panama hat while doing the rounds of Scharloo. He daubed his cheeks with *eau de cologne* every morning. Most Antillean men customarily used perfumes as an effective means of preventing colds of the nose; but he found the aftershaves his daughters tried to give him as presents repulsive: to him they all smelled of horses. He sprinkled himself with ladies' fragrances.

In the words of Robert Rojer, Jacobo Palm had "the refined and somewhat subdued elegance of an officer from the old school." It was therefore no coincidence that a framed picture of his father Manuel hung above his piano, clad in the uniform of a non-commissioned officer trimmed with gold. He, the professional soldier, was the Palm who avoided going down a certain street so as not to embarrass the man who owed him money.

Jacobo (1887–1982) always bowed slightly whenever he shook someone's hand—not just when greeting the governor or the bishop, but also a friend he ran into on the street or when he saw his grandson Robert after another long stint of living in the Netherlands. On the day of his wife's funeral he was the last one to say farewell, before the coffin was closed. As he took her hand and kissed it, he bowed deeply to her, holding his other hand on his back. Robert Rojer: "It took my breath away. I saw the same astonishment all around me. Everyone attending the funeral was transcended into another era. The scene was pervaded with an unexpected sense of lightness; I expected the opening chord of *Eine Aufförderung zum Tanz* to resound at any minute. He said goodbye to his Lisa in a way that was just as gallant and fond as it had been when he had first met her some sixty-five years earlier."

She was once the prettiest girl in Otrobanda. According to Jacobo, that is, though quite a few people agreed. Elisa, the oldest of the four Snijders daughters, had dark eyes and an exceptionally light complexion. In contrast, the third sister Clarita had extremely light, gray-green eyes and an olive complexion. During the time when Robert Rojer had been a physician in Otrobanda, he had heard the old people say that in the decade between 1910 and 1920 people had to express their preference between Elisa with the dark eyes or Clarita with the light ones. Elisa did not use any makeup; Clarita was stylish, a coquette. Elisa would go down in history as the woman who prayed the rosary while watching adulterous relationships unfold on Venezuelan *telenovelas*, Clarita as the unattainable beauty who inspired talented cabinetmakers to make handsome pieces of furniture, poets to write odes, and composers to pen waltzes and mazurkas. As a girl Clarita had been close to death on several occasions; she always made a miraculous recovery. When she felt death was approaching she handed out her jewelry to friends and acquaintances, but asked for it back immediately at the slightest sign of recovery. At age twenty she amazed all the eligible bachelors by taking vows; for the next fifty years she lived in the Sint-Elisabeth Hospital as a member of the Franciscan nuns. And yet she remained a coquette to her dying day. Jacobo Palm dedicated the mazurka *La Encantadora* to her: The Temptress, The Siren. One of the more morbid examples of her eccentricity was Bishop Verriet's kidney stones, which she kept in a bottle.

Elisa—Jacobo called her Lisa—was more down-to-earth. She could lose her temper and fly off the handle. Jacobo always had a good laugh at her, but never in her presence. In any case, he laughed softly, just like he spoke. "Lisa is angry," he chuckled to his grandson Robert, wiping away the tears of laughter with his handkerchief. But when she really did get beside herself with anger and the tone of her voice turned nasty, he would say: "Goodness me, would you look at the time. I really ought to be going, I have to be somewhere."

Jacobo did not keep a mistress. This was a rare thing in the Caribbean islands; all his friends had extra-marital relationships. As far as that was concerned, he was the odd man out. As a young man, he had sown his wild oats, but from the moment he laid eyes on Lisa, he lost interest in all other women. He stayed in love with her his entire life; everything she did fascinated him, everything she said amused him.

After the birth of his children he took offence at the habit of Antillean fathers of seeking sexual pleasures outside the home. Liquor made him mean, rather than happy (he only drank a glass of whiskey to wash down a disappointment) and adulterous relationships filled him with disgust. He finally became so puritanical that he refused to play anything by Brahms because of his affair with Clara, Robert Schumann's wife.

His behavior had to be beyond reproach in order to protect his privileged position. From 1914 to 1966 he was the organist at Sint-Anna Kathedraal (St. Anne's Cathedral) and from 1919 to 1940 music instructor at the Colegio del Sagrado Corazón (College of the Sacred Heart) run by nuns. The girls' boarding school housed in the Habaai country estate was known throughout Latin America as the most chic finishing school of them all. The sisters from Roozendaal all came from the highest echelons of society; they resided with butlers in the Casa Blanca adjacent to the Habaai buildings, taught in Spanish or English, and turned into tyrants at the merest hint of any possible improprieties among the students or faculty. This was to the intense satisfaction of Venezuelan, Colombian, and Peruvian generals, owners of large estates, bank directors, government ministers, and presidents who sent their daughters to school in Curaçao in the first place to safeguard them from possible assassination or kidnapping attempts, and in the second place to make sure they would come home just as chaste as they had left.

The sisters of Roozendaal paid Jacobo Palm a generous salary and had him picked up every morning and brought home every afternoon in a chauffer-driven car. The chauffer often had to wait; even though Jacobo would rise early enough to limber up at the piano, his morning ritual of personal grooming often lasted longer than expected. By the time the Model T Ford finally whizzed its way through Otrobanda, its citizens wondered who had just gone by: Shon Coco the composer or the governor.

Besides being the perfect gentleman at Habaai, two of his daughters were residents at its boarding school, an honor extended to only a select group of girls from the island. The school tuition cost a fortune.

To placate the nuns, Jacobo refrained from attending meetings of the Freemasons. He was the only Palm who was sober at early morning mass on Christmas Day in St. Anne's Cathedral. The other Palms had celebrated Christmas Eve at the Masonic lodge, having liberally partaken of libations, and at four o'clock in the morning they stumbled up the steep spiral staircase that led to the chancel. Swaying in their seats, they played variations on "Silent Night" for organ and strings. The only Palm who sat perfectly still was the organist Jacobo, "so still," the other Palms said, "that you could have stood a glass of water filled to the brim on his head."

The sun rose, and the cathedral bathed in a sea of light. The atmosphere was high-spirited, festive, worldly. Once the service was over, Jacobo made his way across the square to Sint-Elisabeth Hospital, where he accompanied a choir of nuns. Then the third church service, this time a Protestant one in the Sailor's Home, he went accompanied by a physician. For the most part there were Norwegian sailors who had drunk themselves into a state of delirium tremens on Christmas Eve, and they cried out their feelings of loneliness during the Christmas service. The doctor had to give a shot to the worst of them to calm them down, jabbing the needle straight through the fabric of their trousers.

Jacobo did not care about money. He considered the biggest difference between Antilleans and Dutchmen to be how detached they could be when it came to material possessions. He had to laugh at the stinginess of a doctor in the Dutch Navy. Dr. Aarts had paid a house call to the Palm residence clad in his impeccably white dress uniform. After the medical consultation he was paid in cash; a ten-cent piece had fallen to the floor and rolled under the bed. Like a swan that sheds its stately deportment when a piece of bread is thrown into the water, Dr. Aarts crawled on all fours under the bed in search of the errant coin. He emerged a moment later with filth smudged on the jacket and trousers of his uniform, holding the coin triumphantly aloft. For the life of him, Jacobo could not understand why anyone would want to besmirch such an impeccably white uniform for the sake of a pittance.

In a certain sense, that was easy for Jacobo to say; he was married to a woman of means. Lisa's father had a schooner that regularly sailed to South America and earned him a fortune; he owned quite a few splendid houses in Otrobanda and a country estate called Zegu. Moreover, from an early age Jacobo had been a much sought-after and well-paid musician. He had taken on the responsibility of providing for his mother and brothers and sisters when his father died just before he had turned twenty. He postponed his own marriage for a couple of years until he had paid off the family mortgage. He never breathed a word to anyone about that momentous decision—he was straining at the leash to share his bed with Lisa.

He never spoke about money. Money was just not a subject worth talking about, quite simply because it was outside the scope of his interests. Other composers were continually concerned about their income, but not him. Family tradition prescribed that its members live soberly yet be generous. Jacobo became a father to four daughters and one son. To him it was nothing to worry about; he believed that a newborn child meant a new source of income. Or as he himself once put it: "Every child brings its own bread." Robert Rojer had been under the impression that his grandfather had coined the phrase himself, until he read forty years later in Gabriel García Márquez's book *Living to Tell the Tale* that his mother had used the exact same words: "*Mi madre cree que cada niño traia su propia pan bajo el brazo.*" Apparently, it was an expression that stretched from Curaçao to far beyond the coast of Colombia, and which was part of a Caribbean view of life.

Due to his education at the Colegio San-Tomás, Jacobo spoke fluent Spanish, English, and French. He alternated giving music lessons at Habaai in Spanish and English. He named the mazurka he wrote and dedicated to his students *Morning Greetings*. He confided to his friend Bram Capello that he had written the mazurka because he had been charmed every morning by the fresh smell of soap exuded by the girl students during the first lesson of the day. Smells were something that truly fascinated him. Robert Rojer told me: "With Jacobo you always had to follow a line of reasoning to its logical conclusion, since he also meant something by what he did not say. We may therefore assume those students to whom he gave lessons later on in the day did not smell fresh."

Jacobo had his first flute and theory of harmony lessons from his grandfather Gerry. He had just learned how to read and write. Later, when he had become a much sought-after music teacher himself, parents often asked him when it was best to start giving children music lessons. He invariably gave them the same answer: "Just as soon as they have learned how to read and write, because then they can understand the function of what a symbol or sign is that refers to something else." You could not exactly call him a self-taught musician; throughout his entire childhood he took four two-hour music lessons a week. His knowledge of harmony took on mythic proportions; he could transpose every conceivable key on sight. Most professional musicians are perfectly satisfied at being able to transpose a known melody into another key that is not too difficult. Jacobo was able to transpose a melody into any key desired even if he was seeing it for the first time.

The singer Irma Römer had just completed her studies at the conservatory in Puerto Rico. She returned to Curaçao and wanted to let her family, friends, and the local musicians hear what she had learned. Jacobo accompanied her at the concert she gave in the union building of the Asosiashon di Músiko. For her final piece she had chosen an aria from César Franck's *Judith et Holofernès*. She was supposed to start singing after a few opening chords on the piano. Scared out of her wits, she went off the rails right after singing the first notes; her voice slipped into an entirely different and totally wrong key. Jacobo had no problem dealing with it; he slipped right along with her, and the rest of the oratorio was played in the transposed key. No one there noticed, not even the professional musicians.

He had strong views. "Most musicians," he said to his pupil and grandson Robert, "have the tendency of playing passages they do not know well too hard and too fast. It would be more logical to play them more slowly and softly." Or: "This is one of Chopin's more difficult passages. If you think it is difficult, Chopin probably thought it was too. As a composer, Chopin had the liberty of getting rid of it; yet he chose not to do so. We may therefore assume that he was extremely fond of that passage and regarded it as a highpoint. And so that's how you ought to play it: with great care. Take all the time you need, for it is a pivotal point on which the entire piece of music hinges."

You could almost say he had taken lessons from Chopin himself, for, as Benita Eilser has written: "Chopin was a brilliant teacher. He had the gift of being able to impart what he knew to his students in such a way it both freed and inspired them."

Naturally, Jacobo gave lessons on a Pleyel, *the* piano for an Antillean waltz or mazurka. One day not a single sound came from his instrument; it turned out to have been devoured by an army of white ants. With the help of violinist Jacobo Conrad he turned the instrument upside down and drenched it with turpentine. The experiment was a success; all the white ants drowned in the sea of turpentine. But when put the Pleyel back on its legs a few days later, still no sound came out. The ants had silenced the instrument once and for all.

The turpentine-scented Pleyel would remain in Jacobo's house, alongside the Hardman and Peck he bought later. Jacobo used the old piano as a sideboard; after all, you did not just get rid of a Pleyel.

There is also a story to tell about the Hardman and Peck.

A certain Antonio Boom inherited a fortune somewhere around 1910. In good Antillean fashion he came up with a plan to blow it all in one big blast in Paris. On the outward-bound leg of his voyage, the ship taking him to Paris called at New York. While there, Antonio Boom bought a Hardman and Peck, one of America's better brands of piano. The party in Paris lasted six months. Boom's unconcern was so great that he did not give a moment's notice to how he would have it sent home. In order to be able to afford shipping it, he had to work quite a few months in the Gillette razorblade factory in Paris.

When he finally arrived in Willemstad, he found the Hardman and Peck had already arrived. Looking for a buyer, he called together the entire Palm extended family, and they were extremely enthusiastic about the instrument.

The piano ended up in Jacobo's house next to the forever silenced Pleyel. But it was Rudolf who jotted down the details about Antonio Boom in a book about pianos, alongside his notations about the Hardman and Peck brand. The book would remain in the Palm family. For nothing gets lost in the Antilles, except the wind.

16

Celebratory and Elegiac Waltzes

Most waltzes by Antillean composers were commissioned. If you wanted to please someone on Curaçao or Aruba, you gave them a waltz as a gift. The tradition began at the end of the nineteenth century and would continue throughout the whole of the twentieth century.

A few friends of the renowned local writer Boeli van Leeuwen asked Edgar Palm to compose a waltz for his fiftieth birthday. They did not give him a bottle of whiskey or a bunch of flowers; instead they gave him the sheet music to a waltz called *Bouquet*. It was customary to play it in public for the first time at the birthday party, although this did not at all mean it was merely an occasional piece of work. *Bouquet* remained on Edgar Palm's repertoire for years to come and became one of his most popular pieces.

The tradition had by no means disappeared by the time I settled on Curaçao. I attended the celebrations given to commemorate the poet Nydia Ecury's seventy-fifth birthday. Many colleagues had written her poems; others recited by heart poems Nydia had written herself. As the evening progressed, everyone started getting restless. When is it going to happen?, everyone seemed to be asking themselves. A huge sigh of relief went through the house when Wim Statius Muller took his place behind the piano and started playing the waltz he had written especially for the poet, naturally entitled *Nydia*. The party would not have been complete without the waltz.

If you were musically inclined, you could even come up with a melody for a waltz yourself. You then went to a composer, played the tune and asked him to arrange it. For a small fee, he got to work and wrote down the notes. There are hundreds of such scores in the attics of Otrobanda, affairs of the heart that usually bore the name of the person being worshipped and adored.

You were truly noble if you gave someone a waltz, as noble as a true blue Antillean. Paul Quirino de Lima's waltz *¿Por qué sufrir?* became one of the most renowned Antillean waltzes at the end of the nineteenth century. To learn how to play piano, the penniless Paul Quirino had used a slat of wood on which he had painted the black and white keys. Music, he figured, was the only way to reach his cousin Irma. With the money he earned from his first performance he bought a piano. He married the Venezuelan Josefita Sintiago but remained madly in love with Irma. He went on a ride with her every evening in a horse-drawn public tram, to the end of the line in Monte Verde. He asked her to sing; her high, light voice transported him into seventh heaven. He composed *Why Suffer?* in gratitude for all those highly romantic rides.

Not all waltzes were composed solely because of love; for composer Emilio Naar (1876–1945) the reason had been a stomach ache. One of his most famous waltzes was entitled *Botica Central*. The musician's stomach was bothering him after a late-night show at which the liquor had flowed profusely. Early that morning he paid a visit to a pharmacy called *Botica Central*. No one opened the door. Emilio grabbed his violin and made up a waltz right then and there. The pharmacist woke up, and when Emilio told him that he had started playing out of pure misery, not only did he get the best stomach pills money could buy, but also the commission to write out the score of the waltz. Before he went home to sleep it off, Emilio scribbled the notes down on the prescription slips.

Another reason to compose a waltz might just as well have been grief. Music can be heard at all times in Curaçao, and certainly at funerals. Edgar Palm composed the waltz *Padú* for the funeral of the father of the Aruban composer and pianist Padú del Caribe. He was returning the favor since Padú del Caribe had composed a waltz when Edgar's father Shon Dòdò Palm had passed away.

The elegiac waltzes are not that much different from the celebratory ones. All Antillean waltzes are melancholic by nature. It is part and parcel of the atmosphere the islands exude. Whoever watches the final rays of the sun sink beneath the horizon over the immense ocean cannot help but be filled with melancholy. In the classic poem "Atardi" (Dusk), which every Curaçaoan knows by heart since the first line of verse is so melodious in their native Papiamentu language, the poet Corsen asks himself whether he too will set with the sun. The feeling of life's transience never leaves a Curaçaoan, and in the absence of seasonal change he projects that feeling on the *atardi*, the final hour before sunset in which darkness falls with the speed of a change of scenery.

During funeral ceremonies, a waltz is sometimes played that had been composed for the deceased several years earlier. The sociologist René Römer, a full professor at Groningen University and former governor of the Netherlands Antilles, was given a waltz entitled *René* as a present for his seventieth birthday, which was just as sparkling as the twinkle in his eyes. When he passed away five years later, the same waltz was played at his funeral by Wim Statius Muller. No one in attendance was bothered by the effervescent sound of chords that echoed the cheerful tone and rapid speech of the professor; they smiled, and kept time with the beat with a finger, a hand, or a foot.

In Europe, music found its way into the concert hall at the end of the nineteenth century. In the Antilles, music remained close to the people, heard at celebrations and parties, weddings and gatherings, commemorative events and funerals.

Or in moments of dissension.

With the advent of the millennium close at hand, the family Moreno asked itself, while sitting down to Sunday dinner, how the Antillean waltz would develop in the twenty-first century. The discussion was heated and finally they decided to get an expert's opinion. The then ninety-two-year-old Edgar Palm was commissioned to write a visionary waltz. Palm cashed the check and got to work. The result was the waltz entitled *2000*, in which he practically dispensed with the melody altogether and accentuated the rhythm.

It would not have surprised Edgar Palm in the least to have received the commission from a Jewish family. Antillean classical music relied more heavily on the generosity of patrons than European classical music. Most support was given to Antillean composers by the old Sephardic families. For instance, a bequest by Rebecca

Maduro established the S. E. L. Maduro Music Foundation, which released CDs by Edgar Palm, Livio Hermans, Harold Martina, Wim Statius Muller, and Robert Rojer.

Curaçao had been in Spanish hands before it became a Dutch possession. When Johan van Walbeeck set sail in 1634 to conquer the island, he took with him from Amsterdam a Sephardic Jew by the name of Samuël Coheno who could act as interpreter during the negotiations to determine the articles of surrender. Coheno subsequently settled on Curaçao and within twenty years there were twelve Jewish families on the island: Aboab, Cardoze, De Chavex, Henriquez Coutinho, Jessurun, De Leon, Marchena, De Meza, De Olivièra, La Parra, Pareira, and Touro. You can see all these names to this day in the Curaçao telephone directory.

After the seizure of Recife, Johan Maurits van Nassau employed the same tactic; he had as many Sephardic Jews from Amsterdam emigrate as possible to make it easier to maintain contact with the Portuguese planters already there. When the Portuguese reconquered northern Brazil from the Dutch, most of the latter fled to Curaçao.

In 1652, the governors of the Dutch West India Company decided to grant the Jews complete religious freedom. The Mikvé Israël congregation was founded two years later, the Hope of Israel. At first, the Sephardic Jews worshipped in private houses; in the eighteenth century they raised money to build a synagogue. Until the end of the nineteenth century, the official language of the synagogue remained Portuguese.

Curaçaoan Jews applied themselves to the worlds of shipping, commerce, and banking. They participated in funding the revolutions on Cuba, Santo Domingo, and Haiti while also making loans to the conservative opposition. Since they set the same conditions to both parties—a fourfold return on investment should they be victorious—they never made a loss.

Charles Maduro (1883–1947) combined making money with making music. He excelled at doing both. He was managing director of the Maduro & Curiel's Bank, played piano and violin, and composed music. In 1927 he left for New York, where the family opened a branch office of the bank. He kept on composing. The New York music publisher Flaschner & Co. published several of his works, and in 1931 the Manhattan Symphony Orchestra put his

Scherzo Espagnole and *Rhapsodie Espagnole* on their repertoire. The pieces were not all that Spanish, but a title like *Scherzo Curaçaolienne* would not have gone down very well in New York.

The entire Maduro family was musical. Monti Maduro, Charles's brother, played cello, his sister Ida piano and contrabass, and another sister Rebecca composed a couple of lovely waltzes for piano, including the *Souvenir d'un rêve*, which was published in New York, again by Flaschner & Co. Rebecca also wrote a march for her son George, who had been killed in 1940 at the Battle of Grebbeberg on the Dutch border with Germany at the outset of World War II, and who would later become famous in the Netherlands because of Madurodam, the amusement park in The Hague of miniature buildings, which had been named after him.

I suspect that Arthur Rubinstein had stayed with the Maduro family in their magnificent home in Scharloo. The island's second Pleyel grand piano was in Charles's house (the first one had been in the Freemasons' Lodge). The Maduro salon had a magnificent panoramic view of the Waaigat. It was the ideal spot to rehearse new repertoire.

Maduro probably met Rubinstein in New York. Charles was a happy-go-lucky and well-groomed gentleman (a dead ringer for American president Harry Truman) who easily made contacts. He spent a lot time with the then world famous singer Maurice Chevalier, a popular guest in the high society circles Rubinstein also adored frequenting, certainly in Manhattan.

Charles constantly shuttled back and forth between the metropolis and his native island. None of New York's frenetic energy can be heard in his musical works; the waltzes he wrote were virtually indistinguishable from those of his Curaçaoan contemporaries and sounded completely Antillean. The only difference was that in 1935 he orchestrated one of his waltzes in the hopes the Manhattan Symphony Orchestra would include it in their repertoire. He no longer made any attempt to make a Spanish impression and named the waltz *Curaçao*.

The Maduro family served as a model for the Jewish families in Scharloo. Their children took lessons from local musicians; the parents commissioned pieces from Antillean composers or hired them for performances. Not a Jewish feast or wedding ever took place that did not have waltzes and mazurkas—Antillean waltzes and mazurkas, that is.

For Curaçaoan Jews, the promised land was the place in which they had been living since the seventeenth century. The only reference to Israel was the sand from the Sinai desert that had been strewn, a foot deep, across the floor of the synagogue.

17

Shon May and Shon Max

Once a month I used to take a drive to the middle of the island to the plantation house Bloemhof in the Mahaai district. I paid a visit late on those Friday afternoons to see Max Henríquez and his wife May Henríquez-Álvarez Correa. At the time, they were already in their eighties.

They were not really keen on having contact with Dutch nationals; in the days of Shell Oil they had continually been disappointed. "As soon as you had gotten to know a lovely couple," Shon May told me, "you found yourself waving goodbye to them on the quayside." The longest posting for Shell senior personnel in foreign service was two three-year contracts.

The reason they received me as a guest had to do with where I had gone to study—Bordeaux—and the language we spoke. Shon Max had been born in Caracas, went to boarding school in Paris, and studied at the Ecole des Mines. He spoke fluent French, Spanish, and English, reasonable Papiamentu, and not a word of Dutch. He was delighted at being able to converse in French again.

In the early 1950s he had spent a couple of months in Paris with Shon May. She had made sketches, paintings, and sculptures and taken lessons from Zadkine.* Paris was unmistakably part of a delightful carefree period in their lives. Whenever we spoke French together, they were quite animated and suddenly looked much younger than their years.

Shon May owned shares in Maduro & Curiel's, the bank that has branch offices in every neighborhood in Curaçao, Aruba and Bonaire. She must have been quite wealthy. You could not tell by her appearance or by the house in which she and Max lived. Their modestly furnished bungalow was next to the Bloemhof, a small plantation house. Max used one of the side wings as his workspace, while

May used the coach house as her studio. There was nothing luxurious about the residence, that is, in comparison to the American-looking interiors I had come across elsewhere in Santa Rosa. The real money hung on the walls.

Shortly after World War II, Sandberg had been invited to Curaçao by Chris Engels. The young Willem Sandberg, Esquire, who would later make history as the great champion of modern art, had just been appointed director of the Stedelijk Museum in Amsterdam. Engels was a physician, painter, poet, author, pianist, composer, fencing master, and since 1944 the founder of the Curaçao Museum. He was planning on assembling a collection of modern art that would overshadow every other museum from Caracas to California. That would have been possible; in the forties Curaçao was flush with money, and at the time on the international art market you could acquire a Picasso or a Matisse for a mere thousand dollars. At Sandberg's recommendation, Engels also invited another prominent figure: Gerrit Rietveld. The architect provided a monumental staircase for Engel's residence, Stroomzigt, on the Rif section of coastline at Otrobanda, supervised the renovation of the Curaçao Museum, and designed the Monseigneur Verriet Institute for handicapped children. It would become one of the last and most beautiful examples of modern Dutch architecture in the tropics.

As if there were no end to the fun, Sandberg agreed to organize a Van Gogh exhibition at the Curaçao Museum. In 1948 every Van Gogh work the Stedelijk Museum either owned or had on loan was put on display in the Curaçao Museum. Owing to the extreme heat and the threat of the frames warping due to the high humidity, the shutters to the museum were left wide open at night. Thieves could quite easily have leapt over the windowsill at a single bound and plucked the paintings off the walls; there were no guards, and none of the works was attached to an alarm system.

May was on the board of the Curaçao Museum. She became friends with Sandberg, who in 1948 once again came for an extended visit to Curaçao. He introduced her to Zadkine, wrote letters to her regularly informing her of the latest and rapidly changing developments in postwar art, and gave her advice on the acquisition of paintings.

On their walls hang the early works of Karel Appel, Corneille, Lucebert, one of Jan Wolker's first hanging objects (he too had taken lessons from Zadkine in Paris), and a few works by Charles Eyck, who at Sandberg's expense had travelled to Curaçao to weather a mental crisis and took up residence in a small house on the premises of the Curaçao Museum. In the yard were several sculptures by Zadkine and May herself, and by the Curaçaoan artists Hortence Brouwn and Yubi Kirindongo. In the bed and guestrooms hung a selection of Venezuelan art ranging from the sweet pastoral to raw Surrealist styles.

Shon May invariably wore a billowing summer dress and Shon Max a *guayabera*, a shirt made of white linen without lapels. He always greeted women with a kiss of the hand, but without the lips actually touching the skin, in keeping with courteous nineteenth-century etiquette. On May and Max Henríquez's porch, I could quite easily imagine how elegant Curaçao must have been in a bygone era.

May had spent her childhood in Scharloo. From 1860 onward, nearly every wealthy Jewish family lived there, in residences that were practically palaces requiring large staffs of domestic servants to keep them clean and in good repair. By the mid-twentieth century, that lifestyle had become too costly, even for the rich families. Moreover, the local Jewish community became terribly alarmed once the scope of the Holocaust had sunk in. Scharloo had always been a prominent neighborhood, never a ghetto; nevertheless all the Jews lived there crowded together, and under certain circumstances that could be hellishly dangerous. In 1946 and 1947 the Jewish families began dispersing over the entire island.

Jews had never been oppressed on Curaçao. Right from the seventeenth century onward they had held prominent positions in society, and as the years went by their influence increased. They did, however, remain cautious, exerting influence on local politics from behind the scenes and leaving the establishment of schools and newspapers to the Catholic missionaries.

Shon May belonged to the generation that took on the burden of history. As one of the wealthiest girls on Curaçao she had been raised under strict supervision. She was tutored at home her entire childhood, though not by a Jewish tutor but a Protestant theologian, in order to prevent narrow-minded thinking. Her frame of reference had to be greater than that of her immediate circle; she had to be able to empathize with others of a different persuasion. May was quite fortunate with the Reverend Dr. Eldermans, who not only initiated her in the arts of theology and philosophy but in art itself. He himself was a fervent portrait painter and gave May her first painting lessons.

During the week she received a Protestant education, and despite the fact she seldom if ever went to the synagogue on Saturdays, she nevertheless saw quite a few new faces. She was shocked at the arrival of so many Ashkenazi refugees who had fled from Germany, and realized that they belonged to a condemned people.

For the Sephardic Jews, the exodus had begun much earlier in the sixteenth century, when they had to flee from the Iberian peninsula. What May could not understand was why those Jewish refugees to Curaçao had been involved in the slave trade. The same had held true for the Huguenots. After the termination of the Edict of Nantes in 1685, they had been expelled from France, and quite a few of them had sought refuge in the Dutch Antilles, where they soon ran plantations which in turn yielded vast sums of money owing to slave labor. The Jews limited themselves to keeping house slaves only, but they profited directly from the slave trade, and after 1824, when Jews were given full citizenship rights, they took over six plantations, field slaves and all.

Shon May strove her entire life to rectify that shame. She and her husband Max supported practically every artist of color on the island, be they painters, sculptors, authors, poets, or, of course, musicians and composers. They bought works, commissioned waltzes and dances, and paid the least well off the highest advances. Whenever they received a large group of guests, they hired a pianist or a combo. I heard a great deal of nineteenth-century Antillean music for the first time at Shon May and Shon Max's Bloemhof estate, where they regularly organized meetings, debates, and exhibitions.

Shon May translated Molière's *l'Avare* and Sartre's *Huis Clos* into Papiamentu, to show that it was not just some black gibberish, as the Dutch considered it to be until well into the twentieth century, that it was not a dialect but a fully-fledged language in which full justice could be done to the masterpieces of world literature. She had no doubt whatsoever that it was a Latin-based language. She told me she had spoken Papiamentu at a conference in Paris of Sephardic expert linguists and that they had literally been able to understand her word for word. According to her, the source of the language must have been the Sephardic Jews, that is, the language they spoke in the fifteenth and sixteenth century on the Iberian peninsula. The black intellectuals on the island disagreed: they were of the opinion that the source of Papiamentu lay in the Cape Verde islands, where slaves sometimes had to wait for years before being shipped out to the slave market on Curaçao, and where all that time they had spoken among themselves the coastal Portuguese Creole that had been the *lingua franca* of that era.

I sat listening to Shon May for hours on end, to her soft voice in impeccable French. She sometimes chastised me for consistently using the Dutch word *Papiaments* in all my books, instead of Papiamentu, since after all that was the official name of the language, or the variant Papiamento to refer to the Aruban spelling. I countered by saying that in Dutch we use *Frans* and *Engels* and not *français* or English to denote the languages. She could live with that, although she remained concerned about the condescending attitudes of the Dutch toward Dutch Antilleans.

She often drew parallels between the development of the Dutch Antillean language and Antillean music. Though the origins of Papiamentu may have been among the Sephardic Jews, the language had taken on elements of African syntax and the rapid forms of African speech patterns, much in the same way the waltzes, mazurkas, and contradances on the Antilles had become heavily syncopated until they were scarcely distinguishable from the music to which the slaves had originally danced, such as *tambú*.

To her, Dutch Antillean identity could be found in the Sephardic Jewish, African, European, and South American quadrangle. She would propagate that idea until the day she died. Shon Max passed away in 1995, Shon May in 1999. The Bloemhof was turned into a museum. But for me the real museum had been the porch on which I had had all those conversations with May and Max Henríquez. Nowhere else had I tasted Curaçaoan traditions as potently as I did there.

18

Sensuous Movement

Slaves were forbidden to talk to one another while working on the plantations. They communicated with each other by singing. Nor were slaves allowed to live with one another as families; men and women lived in separate huts. They were, on the other hand, allowed to make babies; after all, that produced little slaves at no extra cost.

During the cutting of the maize, they sang about the hardships they endured and the circumstances in which they lived. To the slaves, song and protest were one and the same.

To give added luster to the New Year or the coming of rain, they danced to the rhythm of the *tambú*, the big drum. Depending upon how lenient their masters were, they either danced on the plantation grounds or at some out-of-the-way place. The dance was also called *tambú*.

Or they danced the *tumba* (a corruption of *diumba*, the name of a Congolese dance), usually on Saturday night, since they did not have to work on Sunday. The tambú came directly to the Dutch Antilles from West Africa, the tumba along a roundabout route via Andalusia, Hispaniola (that later separated into Haiti and Santo Domingo) and Cuba.

Accompanied by hand clapping and two instruments—the iron *herú* and the drum stretched with sheepskin—the tambú was sung and danced. The songs were scarcely different from the ritual singing I had heard in the jungles of equatorial Africa. They reminded me strongly of the *mvett* of the Fang, through its antiphony, the call and response, in which the solo male singer or female singer asks questions that are answered by the choir or bystanders.

Two distinct groups gradually formed among the slaves. Those who lived in town as domestic slaves took on the lifestyle of their masters and became *makamba** *pretus*, or black-whites. Every white family owned four or five slaves who served as coachmen, cooks, gardeners, maid servants, or nursemaids. They were not allowed out on the street after 9 p.m., but during the day they did the shopping at the market or drove the *Shon* to the barracks or government buildings. Their fate was not much worse than those of servants in Europe; they were not free, but neither did they suffer in isolation; they were part and parcel of the whole kit and caboodle that made up a household in the eighteenth and nineteenth centuries. They heard the music of the whites and only turned back into Africans when they told the children the Anansi stories about the big, black spider who was too clever for the lion, snakes, and reptiles. Anansi symbolized the sun; its legs referred to its rays.

The field slaves were a thousand times worse off. They were seldom if ever allowed to leave the plantations. They worked there, lived there, and even if they were seriously ill or on their deathbed, they had to stay put. Their entire existence from cradle to grave took place on the plantation. In cultural terms this meant that after five, six, or seven generations they remained as quintessentially African in their customs and habits as their tribal ancestors who had been taken away in chains from deep in the jungle. The African traditions lived on even after the last slave transport ship entered Willemstad harbor in 1778. A single glance at the mid-nineteenth-century drawings of slave villages reveals round huts with thatched roofs that could just have easily been of villages in the interior of Congo, Angola, Nigeria, Ghana, or Ivory Coast, the countries from which the great majority of Curaçaoan slaves originally came. The belief in spirits, rituals, songs, and dances remained totally African. Or to be more precise, it remained true to its origins in the huge area in West Africa that stretches from savannahs in the south of the Sahara to the Congo River.

The only thing that was diluted or watered down was the African worship of ancestry. Many field slaves did not know who their fathers were, let alone their grandfathers. They could not conceive of an all-seeing eye of the ancestors—which was such an essential and strongly regulating custom in African society. On the other side of the ocean, Dutch Christians considered the family to be the cornerstone of society; the way they treated the field slaves in the Dutch

West Indies completely destroyed this notion of family. The consequences would be far reaching; right to this very day there are quite a few black families made up of a mother and children, and a father who is either only nominally present or absent altogether.

During slavery, the men were the ones who played the drum and *heru*, while the women poured out their hearts in song. Men and women were in no way inferior to one another, neither while working the land—the men cut the maize, the women tied the stalks in bundles—nor during the rebellious or ceremonial songs. The women had a say in everything. That too would have long-lasting consequences; female singers such as the Curaçaoan Izaline Calister or the Cuban Omara Portuondo come from a long line of tradition.

As with all African dances, tambú was danced separately, while the tumba was danced in couples. To the whites, the tambú especially was considered a dance of the devil. Whenever Monsignor Niewindt, Curaçao's first Catholic bishop, got wind there was tambú dancing going on during his long horse rides across the island between 1830 and 1860, he headed straight for it with whip in hand. For Niewindt, who had a preference for preaching about chastity, the movements of the hips were so shocking that he had to close his eyes before digging his spurs into his steed.

Even though the man and woman do not touch during the tambú, they move more provocatively than the average Dutch couple while making love. The Curaçaoan poet Pierre Lauffer pulled out all the stops of the Papiamentu language to put the erotic character of the dance into words.

Kanga bo saya
Dui, mi korona
Kokobiá tumba
Te mardugá.

Yanga, mi skèrchi
Di pura stabachi;
Zoya, mi bichi
Bo kurpa ankrá.

Fa'bo kustia
Mucha djingueli;
Balia, mi prenda,
Lagami morcha.

Lift up your skirt
My big foxy lady
Buck the *tumba*
Deep into the night

Swish your hips
Pitch-black bird
Twirl, my worm
Your sturdy body

Gird tight that belt
Around your loins, my naughty one
Dance with me, darling,
Until I drop.

Lauffer (1920–1981) made rewarding use of Papiamentu's short syllables and replicated the exact meter of the tumba the popular Afro-Curaçaoan rhythm similar to tambú. The first three lines of each stanza had precisely the same stomping beat while the fourth line was given a metrical acceleration, as it were.

You can hear the drums playing in his poetry; you can see the women.

There she comes, the Queen
swaying her royal bottom;
undulating behind her—immense—
sensuous movement,
stiffening into streams of sugar
and molasses . . .

Surface to surface
You squeeze rhythm upon rhythm

And sweat and blood and
Grind and grinding
You DANCE.

Tambú was regarded as an act of moral corruption well into the twentieth century. In 1924 Father Jan Paul Delgeur wrote in his weekly column in the *Amigoe di Curaçao*:

> Every now and then the blackies took out the old African tambour in the darkness of night, uncorked a demijohn of rum, and the filthy business began. That vexed me, that repeated foul can-can. What happened then I honestly do not know, but I can still see myself, sinewy six-legged creature that I was, mounted high on my skittish stallion suddenly leaping into the throng of that babbling, hip-swaying, dead drunk negro trash, mercilessly lashing out with my horse whip, with the wondrous effect that in a minimum of time, in that corral impregnated with sweat, stench and banging African sounds, the intense pious silence of a moonlit tropical night once more reigned supreme.

In 1936 the Colonial Council formally declared the dance illegal.

The attorney René Rosalia wrote his dissertation on tambú. He critically examined every piece of legal legislation and governmental decree and came to the conclusion that the colonizer had not taken the slightest interest in fundamental human rights in its crusade to outlaw the dance. In the end, even the elders came to believe they were actually committing a crime by dancing the tambú; after all, you could be arrested for doing it.

The tolerance for which Curaçao was famous only applied to the whites. South American rebels were free to print their subversive writings in Willemstad, but the black population had no freedom of speech, freedom of assembly, or freedom of movement.

Rosalia defended the tambú as the purest form of Afro-Curaçaoan folk art. He even went so far as to reject the idea that the tambú was an erotic form of dance. From the very beginning, he claimed, the tambú served as an incantation and purification ritual. In a physical way, the dancers compelled happiness, health, fertility, or rain (while the choir sang *tambú ta lòs awa* [tambú brings much water]) or warded off the fear of disaster, sickness, and death. Tambú is danced especially in the weeks just before the New Year. The dancers wanted to settle accounts of the previous year on the eve of the New Year, experiencing sweat and trance as a form of purification. They burned incense after the dance to drive away evil spirits and bad influences (*fuku*) from their huts. At the stroke of midnight, they jumped into the ocean. Tambú formed a permanent part of their purification rituals.

But all this did not make the tambú a chaste form of dance. The characteristic thing about African religions is that they do not make a distinction between body and spirit, between instinct and faith, between the conscious and subconscious. In the African way of seeing, everything is one, just as the tambú itself is the beats of the drum, the song, dance, and faith all rolled into one.

Tambú was a way to release pent-up anger, urges, fears, physical lust, desires, and violence. The dance was interrupted by a stick fight between two men. The winner was the one who first wounds his opponent. Blood must flow from the wound, and the loser of the duel lets it drip onto the drum. The drummer then transforms the evil blood into pure sounds.

The lyrics to tambú songs often contained unrelenting protest, even after the abolishment of slavery. Criticism was directed at everything that was wrong within and outside one's own circle. The solo female singer indicates a man as the father of a child; the bystanders answer.

> SOLO: You have given me a bad name.
> CHORUS: Liar of a man.
> SOLO: You say the child isn't yours.
> CHORUS: Liar of a man.
> SOLO: But you were the lover.
> CHORUS: Liar of a man.
> SOLO: Now the child is here you deny it.
> CHORUS: Liar of a man.
> SOLO: But bad luck to you, the child is your spitting image.
> CHORUS: Liar of a man.

Tambú singers point an accusing finger at the local potentate—the governor—or at the oil refinery, which did not instigate accident insurance until 1938 and a health care plan until 1941.

A very popular tambú song in the early forties was called *Hitler*:

> *Hitler a laga sa*
> *Ku su bandera tin kurá munder rònt*
> *Antoe bandera no ta sirbi*
> *Ni pa paña di seka mal muhé*
>
> Hitler declared his flag
> Would be flying all over the world
> But his flag isn't even fit
> As a beach towel for the naughtiest woman

But the members of the Colonial Council ignored the lampoonish character of the tambú and banned the dance.

The oldest ban against freedom of assembly, "with or without contrabasses, violins or guitars," dates from 1710. Since then there had been a long series of decrees, statutes, regulations, and ordinances culminating in a legal ban on Bonaire in 1935 and Curaçao in 1936.

The Colonial Council was not made up solely of Dutch civil servants. The governor—a Dutch national appointed by the Dutch Crown—was allowed to appoint five members of the Curaçao elite at his own discretion; moreover, in the twentieth century ten council members could also be elected. Universal suffrage would not come into effect until 1948; those eligible to vote were well-to-do Protestant and Jewish citizens. Among those who voted for Article 36 of the General Police Statutes—"it is forbidden to organize a dance or participate in one where a tambour dance is held"—were J. C. Henriquez, J. W. J. van der Linde Schotborgh, R. R. Muskus, A. P. A. van Leeuwen, S. A. L. Maduro, D. Capriles, and S. A. Senior, descendants of prominent Jewish and Protestant families who had been longstanding supporters of Dutch Antillean music. According to the minutes of the hearing, only D. Capriles offered any form of protest: "Mr. Chairman . . . This type of dance is seriously on the wane . . . it won't be long before it dies out altogether." But even David Capriles, father of the pianist Harold Martina who would later rise to fame, in no way wished to "break a lance for this less than ennoble form of dance." In the end, he demurred and voted in favor of the ban.

The other men kept silent and raised their hands in favor when it came to a vote: S. A. Senior, whose father had been on the editorial board of *Notas y Letras*; S. A. L. Maduro, whose brother was a composer; A. K. A. van Leeuwen, father of prominent local author Boeli van Leeuwen. Why did they all vote in favor of the ban? Did they have such contempt for the black members of the population?

Yes and no. It is certain that seven members of the Colonial Council conceived children with black women. Their children or grandchildren told me this, the white ones or the brown ones.

Even though they did not legally recognize them as their children, they paid for their educations and child support. A widespread practice among white men was to be initiated in the art of love by black women before they entered into marriage with a Jewish or Protestant young lady of irreproachable repute. The brown children often took on the names of their fathers, with a slight change in spelling to prevent confusion with their legitimate offspring. The bastard children of Pietersz called themselves Pieters, of De Haseth, just Haseth, and of Palm, De Palm or Palma.

Most of the members of the Colonial Council were pots calling the kettle black. When they were young they had danced the tambú or at the very least lusted after the swivelling hips of the black women. Caprile's remark that the dance was a thing of the past was a white lie; he had seen with his own eyes that the dance was very much alive and kicking. The whole discussion was hypocritical.

The gentlemen were under immense pressure. During the nineteenth century, the government authorities had scarcely acted against tambú. The by-laws and ordinances were merely for appearances' sake; in practice they were dead letters of the law. The owners of the largest plantations of Savonet, San Juan, and Santa Cruz openly permitted the singing and dancing of tambú. A little fun now and again heightened one's enthusiasm for work, and slaves who danced did not revolt. The owners of San Juan, descendants of the Van der Linde Schotborgh family, were even downright fans of tambú. They not only watched, they joined in the dance.

The Roman Catholic clergymen, on the other hand, were strongly opposed to tambú. Monsignor Niewindt had written in 1850: "What good are all our endeavors to civilize the lower classes, if the authorities publically condone debauchery, offensive sexual acts, drunkenness and voluntarily turn a blind eye to the subsequent disorderliness that arises as a consequence?" According to Niewindt, "the highest authorities liberalized the moral ties with the lower classes and amused themselves during the Christmas holidays amid the staggering, licentious and indecent multitude."

The power of the Roman Catholic Church increased dramatically in the twentieth century. Hundreds of friars and missionaries came to the Netherlands Antilles to set up the educational system and spread the gospel among the black population. The churches shot up from the earth like cacti.

There had been a tacit agreement in the Netherlands that the Protestants would direct their missionary activities at the Indonesian population, while the Roman Catholics would concentrate on converting the black populations of Surinam and the Netherlands Antilles. Until well into the nineteenth century, Calvinists had held sway in the Netherlands, and they had a much higher opinion of the Asian population than of the former black slaves. It was possible to eradicate superstition and animism among the Javanese, Moluccans, and Amboinese, but not the Negroid peoples.

It took half a century after the abolishment of slavery to stamp out illiteracy among the black population of the Netherlands Antilles. Whoever could not read or write was incapable of being confirmed in the Protestant faith. Protestants only baptized the children of parents who had been confirmed; Protestantism remained the faith of the white elite. Protest arose against this from, among others, Minister Conradi, who in 1844 had the Book of Matthew translated into Papiamentu as a prelude to having the entire Bible translated. Nevertheless, coloreds and blacks shrank from entering Protestant churches and Catholic missionaries took on the task of converting practically all the nonwhites to Christianity.

The Roman Catholic clerics all hailed from the countryside of the Dutch provinces of Brabant and Limburg, not from the big cities in North and South Holland. They were a small and narrow-minded folk. The priest at Westpunt broke up a small group of people who were dancing the tambú at home. He grabbed the drum, tied it around the neck of a pig, and drove the animal through the streets of the village. To him tambú was such an indecent and diabolic act that even a pig ought to be ashamed of it.

Even the priests Euwens and Brenneker, whose social work made them well liked among the blacks, had a go at tambú. In the 1930s the clergy decided to root out evil at its source. The blacks did not know any better; it was all the fault of the whites who allowed it to go on. The bishop forced the Colonial Council to take action. He had an important trump card in hand: the Roman Catholic Church paid for practically the entire school system. The influential Jews and Protestants ought to offer something in exchange, and they in turn reasoned that passing Article 36 would not cost a cent.

The war against African dances was being waged throughout the Caribbean. In 1826 the governor of Puerto Rico forbade the *bomba* dance and in 1849 the *merengue*. The colonial authorities in Trinidad banned the calypso-song in 1920 and in 1922 the Cuban government outlawed the *bembé*. You might say that the authorities on Curaçao and Bonaire were a bit late in issuing their prohibitions.

This section of the law had the opposite effect on young people. The dance was more popular than ever, and not just with blacks, but among the coloreds and whites. Whoever danced tambú tasted the forbidden fruit. White girls were given a hiding if their parents found out they had snuck out to dance the tambú.

A black woman called Chumunu organized tambú evenings in the Otrobanda district of the capital Willemstad. She posted doormen at the entrance to keep an eye out on the street and they gave a signal to the drummers whenever they saw the cops coming. As soon as they saw a uniform, they called out the password: "Plantains with green peels." At the time the police had green uniforms. Chumunu's soirées were attended by blacks, coloreds, Jews, and Protestants. So as not to arouse suspicion by the authorities, she asked all the men to come dressed in suits.

The lyrics to tambú songs were raw, hard, critical, defiant; those of the tumba were humorous, teasing, more like texts for cabaret. By the twentieth century the dances all came to resemble one another more and more. "You might say," wrote the poet Pierre Lauffer, "that the tumba is a more polished version of the tambú." Even the texts began to become more similar, even though they always retained something of the character of protest songs.

In the end, the unintended effect of the Roman Catholic clergy was to give this heathen dance a much wider audience. When the

Brabant and Limburg priests brought carnival to Curaçao they brought the devil into the home. The celebration that preceded Ash Wednesday, was not immediately popular on the island; until well into the 1950s it was only celebrated on a small scale. It was not until the great rebellion of the black population in 1969 that it was transformed into a bona fide Caribbean celebration in which the tumba became the center of attention.

Six weeks before carnival explodes, a festival begins that lasts three days and nights. Around one hundred participants sing their tumba, a merry, ironic, or bitingly sarcastic song that comments on the most important events of the previous year. A jury selects the winner. He or she is crowned the King or Queen of Tumba and rides on the most beautifully decorated float during the *gran marcha* or great carnival march. The winning tumba is then the official carnival song and is played hundreds, thousands of times on the local radio stations. By the time carnival has ended every Curaçaoan can dream the lyrics and beat of the song.

19

Max and the Shark

Hortence Brouwn returned from Italy at the end of 1994. I moved from Kaya Tapakonchi, where I had been writing in her atelier, to the south coast at Boca San Michiel, a fishing village ten kilometers from the city. I again heard tambú there, this time being played during a ceremony that was so African I imagined I was on the banks of the Congo River.

The fishermen in Boca San Michiel, or Boca Sami as it is known locally, form an autonomous community. Carnival is never celebrated in Boca Sami; on the last day of April and the first two days of May the fishermen celebrate a harvest festival that begins with a blessing of their fishing boats by the local priest.

Before the road to Willemstad was paved, the women of Boca Sami used to go into town twice a week to stock up on cornmeal. The fishermen only saw the city from the sea and docked at Piscadera Bay only to sell their catch. Seven days a week they plied the waters off the southern coast of the island in their wooden boats, in search of tuna and dradu, a whopper of a fish they catch by hand with fishing rods.

I was told in Boca Sami that at a certain point in time the men were among the first slaves to buy their own freedom. The scorn of their fellow slave brothers was the highest price they had to pay. They were considered showoffs, always doing odd jobs in their little time off just to make a few extra bucks; they were scabs the master could always depend upon. Their isolation lasted long after Emancipation became law, since nothing from the days of slavery was forgotten.

In the mid-nineteenth century, a few whites manned the fort in the bay at Boca San Michiel. One of them, a guardsman named Zimmerman, a German I was told, got married three times—each with black women—and fathered twenty-seven children. In local archives he is known as Christiaan Zimmerman, a military man from the Dutch province of Zeeland, although it is perfectly possible he had become a naturalized Dutch citizen before embarking for the West Indies. At any rate, when I came to live in Boca Sami, every other fisherman there was named Zimmerman.

My neighbor Max Zimmerman was already an old man who still managed to make a living fishing by himself on the sea. His son used to go with him every now and again, not out of necessity but just to have a chat. Max was "somewhere in his eighties." He remarried for the second time at age sixty to an older woman, who, if we are believe him, spoiled him every night like a young girl. She, and the daily dose of sea air, kept Max virile.

He waved at me every morning before setting out. The house I had rented was right on the water; I had breakfast about ten meters above the sea, on a rocky plateau, and followed all the little boats that left the bay, prancing on the choppy waves beyond the surf. Sterns, frigate birds, and pelicans trailed in their wake. Sometimes, when a school of sperm whales was spotted, the boats crisscrossed the water in every direction. One swish of the their tailfins was capable of pulverizing the bow of the little barques.

At the end of the day, Max moored at the dock diagonally below my house. A long flight of stairs, which had been hacked out of the rocks, connected the patio with the wooden platform, supported by four poles in the sea. Max was on the dock, clubbing to death the sea snakes he had just caught. He slid me a piece of the gooey mess that was left, for me to toss in my fish broth. My day began with Max and ended with Max.

On that cool February morning he went to sea with his son. As the small craft, which like most Curaçaoan fishing vessels was six meters long and painted orange and white, cut through the waves Max went about setting his lines. Just below the Bay of Lagun, he hooked a spirited fighter. His son asked him if it was not too heavy for him, but Max shook his head decisively: this sucker is mine. The fight began: a fight that would last a full three hours. He had not hooked a tuna, nor a dradu; Max quickly realized thanks to the spectacular leaps that he had caught a shark, a scoundrel about two meters long. It was a nurse shark, one of those nice ladies that only eat plankton and never attack another fish or swimmer, but who once hooked, become absolutely furious. Max finally got it onboard, which was no mean feat in itself, and he had to dispatch the monster with his knife since it was flailing around and giving as good as it got.

His son told me all this later. After the fight, Max had to sit down on the little stool in the forecastle which the fishermen in Boca Sami call the "the cabinet." He dozed off.

His son had long since started heading back to port when he noticed that there was something wrong with his father's posture, he looked like he was suffering from cramps. Felix hurried to his father and tried to rouse him from sleep, only to discover that he was no longer among the living.

The son put into the bay, pulled the boat ashore, and alerted his fellow villagers. Six fishermen carried him from the boat to his house, catty-corner from mine. Early that evening I was informed that I was expected to attend the wake.

Max lay in state on the front porch of his house. According to Dutch Antillean custom the coffin lay on a bed of ice. Next to him, two yards away, lay the shark, also on a bed of ice. Max and the shark were the exact same length, one meter ninety.

Max's wife sat next to him in an upright kitchen chair. She was not sad. It had been a fair fight with the shark, her husband's final courageous hurrah. She smiled at me: yessir, Max died a brave man.

Death had never seemed so natural to me.

In the same quiet tone of voice she informed me that we were waiting for the drummers, for all three drums who would keep evil spirits at bay all night long. They showed up around midnight.

They took turns playing the *tambú-di-vel,* the muffled mourning drum. The listeners kept time nodding to its rhythm. The women wore bright red dresses, another way of keeping away *fuku,* or evil spirits. The muffled drumbeats resounded until the break of dawn.

At daybreak they put the lid back on the coffin and the six fishermen carried Max to the graveyard. At the head of the procession was the priest from Boca Sami and two altar boys.

Africa at night, Europe in the morning.

After the funeral we ate fish soup, from a traditional Curaçaoan recipe.

20

The Rebels

There is an old photograph of the Palm family taken in 1904. Sitting in a rocking chair on the left is Jan Gerard with a music score on his lap. He is wearing a remarkable piece of headgear, a flat, round black calotte (skull-cap) on his white, bald head to protect it from the tropical sun. A luxuriant beard covers his ears. You could swear it was Tolstoy sitting there, on the front porch of his dacha. Standing next to him is Rudolf, in a black suit and white shirt with high starched collar. John is sitting with a clarinet in his right hand. He is wearing a tuxedo with a black bowtie. Jacobo is standing with a transverse flute in both hands; he too is decked out in a tuxedo, but with a white bowtie. They were impeccably dressed musicians, photographed in front of the piano—proper gentlemen who earned their living playing in the salons of the upper classes. You would not say by looking at them that they were rebels who went against the moral grain that prevailed at the time.

Jan Gerard Palm composed his first tumbas in the 1860s. Slavery had not even been abolished yet; his tumbas constituted open and subversive acts of defiance. The same held true for his not hiding the fact he had relations with a black woman—or perhaps that relationship was precisely what made him side with the rebellious artists.

Fourteen of Jan Gerard Palm's tumbas have been saved for posterity, with such mellifluous titles as *Ranka mina, Jan Schorrenber,* or *Sji Maraja.* The last tumba was practically atonal—yet another act of defiance.

Jules Blasini, Chris Ulder, Joseph Sickman Corsen, Paul Quirino de Lima, José María Emirto de Lima, Jacobo Conrad, and Isaac Alfonso Da Costa Gómez dared not follow in Jan Gerard Palm's footsteps. They played it safe by confining themselves to waltzes and mazurkas, which, no matter how Antillean they may have sounded, bore a European stamp. They dared not commit the sin of dabbling in the devil's dance. Only in the third section of the danza did they cautiously introduce African-related rhythms akin to tambú.

John de Pool, whose memoirs written in Spanish were extremely popular in late-nineteenth-century Curaçao, railed against the African dances: "The tambú is to the quadrille what the vulgar common man is to the aristocrat and the disgustingly putrid hovels of the poor to the gleaming ballrooms of the rich."

Jan Gerard Palm flew straight in the face of the pact the Roman Catholic clergyman and the Dutch colonial authorities had concluded to maintain moral standards.

His sons and grandsons were the only ones to follow in his footsteps: Jacobo and Rudolf Palm composed tumbas. That rhythm was finally incorporated into classical music by their students Julian Basílico Coco and Wim Statius Muller, but not until well into the twentieth century. It was then the Curaçaoan author Boeli van Leeuwen wrote a poem about Jan Gerard the Patriarch.

> He is a Palm
> And in the shade of his blisters
> we have gathered the precious dates:
> delicate waltzes,
> hot-blooded tumbas,
> and courtly mazurkas.
> Music that is ours and ours alone.

Wim Statius Muller told me that his uncle August George—who everybody called Etie—once had something he wanted to discuss with Jan Gerard Palm. While they were having coffee, they were interrupted by an uninvited guest. "Shon Gerry, I need a tumba. Can it be ready by tonight?" Shon Gerry asked if he had lyrics. Yes indeed. "Two or three parts? Two will cost you five guilders, three, seven fifty." "Ok, three. When can I come and get it?" "In an hour." Uncle Etie offered to come back the next day so Palm could work on the tumba without being interrupted, but Shon Gerry said: "No, it's okay, just say what you want to say." All that time he was busy composing the music to the lyrics. Before he was finished the next customer called.

They were usually gossip tumbas. One is about Erani who tells her boss that she is sick and is not able to work. The lyrics insinuate that she is pregnant, though she dares not tell anyone. Gerry Palm wrote tumbas like they were on a conveyor belt, and the one who commissioned the piece put his name on it.

The door was always open at the Palm house: everyone should be able to come at any hour of the day or night. There was always food on the table at the Palms', for late in the evening or in the middle of the night, one must always be able to satisfy his hunger. By everyone, the Palms meant those who bought the tumbas, their friends, the other musicians on the island, and the poets Chal Corsen, Yolanda Corsen, and Pierre Lauffer. They were considered part of the family. And you could always crack open a bottle at the Palm house; they led a bohemian existence.

I went to visit Edgar, the last of the Palm dynasty. He immediately poured us a couple of glasses and asked his wife to heat up some *ayakas*. Antilleans stuff *crêpes* with stewed meat, cooked funchi (cornmeal), raisins, olives, and prunes, pickle them in banana leaves, and freeze them, so they can easily be heated up and served to an uninvited guest. Freida simmered the ayakas in a pan with hot water.

Frieda Palm-Palm. "Yes," Edgar told me, "everywhere you look it's a Palm." Frieda was John's daughter, the clarinet player who contracted tuberculosis. She was a full niece to her husband Edgar.

Edgar knew more about the history of Antillean music than anyone else. He had been commissioned to write its history some thirty years after Boskaljon's lament. In that book, published in 1978, he finally brought the local composers into the limelight and gave his own family pride of place. Rightfully so, but *Muziek en musici van de Nederlandse Antillen* (Music and Musicians of the Netherlands Antilles) would have been even better if an outsider had written it. That did not bother Edgar in the least; he was able to have plenty of pictures from the family photo album appear in print. Photographs fade faster in the tropics than anywhere else, so he had saved quite a few of them for posterity. After all, he did not have to be modest; his book was a treasure chest of information.

Edgar was the first Palm to have furthered his studies in Holland, though not in music. He received a scholarship from the Ministry of the Colonies to study at the Intermediate Technical School in

Haarlem. He took his diploma in 1928 in mechanical engineering. He then applied to the same ministry for a scholarship to study at the conservatory. The ministry contacted the Colonial Council of Curaçao, who rejected the application; the Curaçao government had need of his services at the Department of Public Works. When he returned home to the island he heard he could not even get a job as a street cleaner. He was turned down by Public Works and every other government department.

In 1936 the Colonial Council officially outlawed tambú. Was there a connection here? Not officially, of course. Edgar took it as a warning, a dig at him from someone. The Palms should not get the idea they could get away with anything they pleased. Now that it was official that drum music had been banned, they had to tow the line no matter how popular they were with the locals.

At the time, Edgar had not written any tambús or tumbas. The act of revenge was directed more at his brother Alberto Telésforo Palm (1903–1958), son of Rudolf (Shon Dòdò) who became the most popular Palm among the black population. From the very start his music career began in earnest; he took piano lessons from his father, replacing him at age thirteen as the organist in the Jewish synagogue. However, there was a great shortage of bass players in the local dance orchestras. He then took bass and cello lessons from Paul Quirino de Lima. The arrival of silent films afforded Alberto extra work. He founded an orchestra that accompanied the silent flicks every evening in the Cinelandia movie theatre. That orchestra made him wildly popular with the people. He was also an excellent tambú dancer. He organized tambú parties in the privacy of his home, not open to the public, behind locked doors. He was a thorn in the side of the authorities. For the numerous parties at the Café International, Café Suiza, or El Globo Rojo he composed such prim and proper waltzes as *Aura* and *Anna*; for the get-togethers at home he composed rugged tambús that he played on the piano, with or without a singer. His day job was at Shell Oil. He used to whistle melodies to his tambús on the work floor to check whether ordinary workers liked what they heard. So as not to forget a note, he wrote them down immediately. But he could not use pen and paper, since that could be discovered too easily and he would be fired on the spot. He devised an ingenious system of notating them with punch cards.

Alberto was a rebel, too, and made life really tough for his younger brother. But Edgar did not lose courage. He continued his music studies with his father, gave lessons, played in practically every orchestra in sight and, like his brother, took a job with Shell. In 1949 he asked to take a long leave of absence and enrolled at the Royal Conservatory in The Hague.

His forefathers had all been self-taught musicians; he was determined to get a thorough education in music theory. At age forty-five he was the oldest student at the conservatory. In The Hague he immersed himself in a study of Bartók. Traces of this influence can be heard in the compositions he made in the 1950s. Before that he had composed mainly waltzes, but when he resettled in Curaçao he composed seven tumbas and five ballads for Carlos Sillé's *Ballet Criollo*. In one of the ballads, entitled *Buchi Fil*, he combined Bartók-like hammer blows with tambú rhythms. For a piece of Caribbean music, it is quite long, lasting some seventeen minutes.

With that piece of work, Edgar paid homage to the epic poem by Pierre Lauffer, about the slave Buchi Fil who refused to bow to the master during a morning roll call. The master plots his revenge, fearing the slave's physical strength, and he finally brings him to his knees by selling his beloved Mosa Nena to another master far away. With her name on his lips, Buchi Fil throws himself from the cliffs. Ever since, whenever the wind blows you can hear his voice calling in the hills on the western part of the island: Mosa Nena, Mosa Nena, Mosa Nena.

Buchi Fil was premiered in 1955. By this time, the Colonial Council had been dissolved. In 1954 the Netherlands Antilles gained autonomy in all government departments except defense and foreign affairs. From that moment on, the tambú could be openly played and danced; the prohibition had been rescinded.

The only authorities who continued to object were the clergy. Priests paid regular visits to Edgar. He himself was Protestant, at least nominally, as were most of the Palms. Lutheran by denomination, Freemasons in practice—that was the family tradition for most of the Palms, although some of them converted to Catholicism. When Edgar's mother, a colored woman, had taken her first holy communion, the priests came to have a serious word with him. He did the same with the priests as he had with me: he poured them a drink and asked his wife to heat up the ayakas. He promised to mend his ways after the first glass; after the second glass he promised to compose a pious song for the clergyman. And next season, whether the rainy or dry one, the priest would show up again to give him a sermon since he had not kept either of his promises. After all, a man has a short memory, right?

Rebels. Bohemians. But the Palms remained traditional in one aspect. Jacobo, Rudolf, and Edgar started their days in the exact same way as their Nestor, Jan Gerard. They got up early, just before six, sat down behind the piano, and began playing works by their all-time favorite composer.

A Palm never began the day without Chopin.

21

The New Woman

The first Palm to set foot on the South American continent was killed immediately. The clarinetist George Mount died at La Guaria in 1894, just shy of thirty-five. Ever since then, a Palm would think twice about daring to make the crossing.

None of the Palms studied at the conservatory in Caracas, none of the Palms settled for any length of time in one of the Venezuela's coastal cities. Jules Blasini, Chris Ulder, Jacobo Conrad, and Janchi Boskaljon also avoided the continent. Joseph Sickman Corsen was the only one of the nineteenth-century composers to have spent a number of years in Venezuela.

In spite of this, South American music in general had an unmistakable influence on Dutch Antillean music. In 1929 a record number of 2000 Venezuelans were living as political refugees in Curaçao. The Venezuelans brought their melodies with them and sang them just as passionately as they had around the campfires on the vast plains.

Nevertheless, Dutch Antillean composers avoided the *joropo*, the dance style of the Venezuelan *llaneros*. Dutch Antillean musicians also avoided the harp, the llaneros' featured instrument, which they played in a way they inherited from the local Indians. On balance, they were more inspired by African and European music than South American, which in turn was largely based on Spanish music.

Antillean composers incorporated Spanish rhythms in their waltzes and dances. But the assertion of Hoetink, the founder of Caribbean studies in the Netherlands, that Jan Gerard Palm, Jacobo Conrad, and other nineteenth-century composers had copied the Dutch Antillean waltz directly from the joropo is entirely wrong.

Robert Rojer has listened to thousands of joropos in his lifetime. He considers the differences between the Antillean waltz and joropo to be as "vast as the sky and clear as day." In the joropo, the stress is on the first beat and sometimes, for variety's sake, all three beats get the same stress. In the Curaçaoan waltz the stress is on the first beat and after one and a half beats (exactly halfway through the measure) in such a way as to suggest 2/4 time. Not a single joropo contains that binary measure. To be sure, Jan Gerard Palm, Joseph Sickman Corsen, Jacobo Conrad, and Louis Moreau Gottschalk all stole bits and pieces, but all from one and the same person: Chopin. He was the first one to experiment using the binary measure (2/4 time in a tripartite rhythm) in the waltz.

According to Robert Rojer, the Antillean waltz is more ingenious than the joropo. It is also less joyous, more melancholic, more serious—more European, as they say in Venezuela. But then again, it is more sensuous. And the Antillean waltz leans much more heavily on African dance rhythms.

For more than a century and a half Dutch Antilleans were fearful of cultural and political annexation. That fear was not without reason: Venezuelan dictators considered several times whether or not to annex Curaçao, Aruba, and Bonaire, considering them pirates' nests. On a Saturday evening in 1929, six hundred Venezuelan rebels attacked the Waterfort on Curaçao, ransacked guns and ammunition, and took the governor and military commanders as hostages on a confiscated ship bound for Venezuela. The scoundrel Rafael Simón led the attack; his second-in-command was the communist lawyer Gustavo Machado, who was planning a revolutionary coup d'état. The attempt to overthrow dictator Juan Vincente Gómez failed; the governor and military commander did not make it out alive, but the islanders were frightened out of their wits. For the time being, the Netherlands did not consider stationing a warship in the Antilles. The lightning strike by the rebels had just gone to show how completely defenseless Curaçao was to any Venezuelan invasion. To be sure, being subjugated by Holland or Venezuela was a choice between two evils, but the islanders did not really have any doubts: they had much less to fear from The Hague, some nine thousand kilometers away, than they did from nearby Venezuela, and though the Netherlands was a colonial bogeyman, it was nevertheless a constitutional state, a democracy. It would take Venezuela until 1959 to achieve a similar status.

Antillean composers adopted the lively Moorish rhythms, but that was the extent of it. After all, they tended more toward the melancholic than the raw passion of the llaneros.

Curaçao and Aruba had strong economic ties with Venezuela. The neighbor to the south had a similar kind of economic relationship with the two islands that the Netherlands had with Germany. Venezuela (four times the size of Germany) was already a moderately wealthy country in the seventeenth and eighteenth centuries, owing to cacao and coffee, and would become substantially wealthy in the twentieth century thanks to the export of crude oil, coal, and iron ore. Quite a few Dutch Antilleans tried their luck in Caracas or Valencia; Venezuela's largest insurance company was owned by a rich Jewish family from Curaçao.

Colombia was farther away, but was considered more refined. Colombians spoke the loveliest Spanish in all of South America, were much more courteous, and were much better read than Venezuelans. A rich Venezuelan drove around in an American gas guzzler, wore a cowboy hat, drank whiskey, and shouted, all of which were anathema to the softly conversing, wine-sipping Colombian.

I once took a trip by sea to Cartagena de Indias in Colombia. From the water the city strongly resembled Venice, and when you go ashore, you would swear by the architecture that you were in Seville or Córdoba. I had not been in the city one hour before a gentleman dressed in a dazzling white suit made my acquaintance and said he would love to show me his collection of pre-Columbian art. Once at his home he asked me which authors I held in greatest esteem, and when I mentioned both García Márquez and Alváro Mutiz, he insisted on treating me to a meal. In Colombia, you speak to college graduates about literature and art; in Venezuela, about money.

In Colombia, an artist is immediately called *maestro* and can expect as much admiration as a trapeze artist in a circus tent. Because of this, this country appealed a great deal more to Antillean composers than did Venezuela. The flutist Juancho Naar, son of the theatre owner Jacob Naar, was the first Curaçaoan musician to seek his fortune in Barranquilla, a rapidly expanding city at the end of the nineteenth century. He quite soon became a music instructor at the local music school and gave concerts throughout Colombia. Emirto de Lima (1890–1972), son of the Curaçaoan composer Paul Quirino de Lima, followed his example. He first went to France, where he completed his studies in piano and violin; returning to the West Indies in 1925, he established himself as a music teacher in Barranquilla. Shortly thereafter, that which every Antillean feared happened. He was completely engulfed by South American culture. Emirto already spoke fluent Spanish and hardly had to make any cultural adjustments—after all, Dutch Antilleans practically live the same way as the average Latin American. But what was more unfortunate was the loss of his distinctive Antillean musical identity. He composed some thirty *pasillos* and at most added a smidgen of virtuosity to that Colombian dance genre. The pupils jostled one another on his doorstep; after all, he was an Antillean, and for a Colombian, Curaçao is already a long way towards Europe; on top of all that he had studied in France. But his compositions lost their typically Antillean character.

In Barranquilla, Emirto had his picture taken in suit and tie with all his decorations pinned on it, one *Gran Cruz* after another, some thirty-five in all. His bearing, too, standing erect with his hands behind his back, lends him something of the appearance of a South American general looking back on three civil wars and an endless succession of battlefields.

He celebrated great successes in Colombia but was completely left out of Antillean music history. To be sure, he too composed waltzes, mazurkas, preludes, impromptus, and nocturnes; one thing he had in common with other Caribbean composers was not being able to shake Chopin's influence. But when he died, the obituaries referred to him as a Colombian composer.

His most famous composition is *La mujer nueva*. "The New Woman" was a composition in nine parts: *la mujer chofera, la amatriz, la tenista, la atleta, la jugadora de bridge, la Yachtwoman, la billarista, la dactilógrafa, la doctora* (the woman chauffer, the amatriz, the tennis player, the athlete, the bridge player, the yachtwoman, the billiard player, the dactilografa, the doctor). The ironic titles are those of an incorrigible macho right out of a short story by García Marquez.

It was no coincidence that García Márquez, when he was a journalist in Barranquilla, often walked past Emirto de Lima's house, in order to hear a few strains of piano. By then, Emirto was already an old man who had decorated the walls of his house with prints of Fort Amsterdam, the Rif, and the Dutch-looking tiled rooftops of Otrobanda.

22

Curfew

Wim Statius Muller drew his childhood on a piece of paper in front of me. He had grown up in Otrobanda, the district of tradesmen and craftsmen that had been built in the eighteenth and nineteenth centuries on the other side of Santa Annabaai. His parental home was at the corner of the Roodeweg and Mgr. Niewindstraat. On the Mgr. Niewindstraat lived Coco Palm, Dòdò Palm, the bassist Albert Palm, the pianist Robbie Rojer, the pianist Chrisma Henriquez, and the Corsen family, offspring of Joseph Sickman Corsen, all of whom played an instrument. All Wim had to do was open the wooden blinds on his bedroom window to hear music and simply cross the street to take piano lessons from Coco Palm.

Born in 1930, Wim grew up in the heyday of Curaçao music. During World War II the oil refineries on Aruba and Curaçao delivered two-thirds of the fuel oil and kerosene for the Allied ships and planes; in economic terms these were prosperous times for the islands. The standard of living shot upward and a long procession of Chevrolets, Pontiacs, and Chryslers crawled through the narrow streets of Punda. There was sporadic danger: German U-boats tried firing on the refineries from the sea. American warships put a blockade around the islands. The four hundred American military personnel stationed on Aruba and Curaçao made sure the lights stayed out all night long. Curfew began right after sundown.

The only form of entertainment the islanders had was music. Pianists, violinists, reedmen, and guitar players all gathered in the houses of Otrobanda to perform for a multitude of people. The composers worked overtime; the demand for new work was huge. As an exception to the rule, even a symphonic work was produced; Dòdò Palm wrote the concert waltz *Elly* and Rudolf Boskaljon composed the *Symphonie Curaçao* on the basis of local folk songs. Both works premiered on June 20, 1944.

Wim Statius Muller experienced everything firsthand, and at fifteen he could not imagine a life without music.

The musician who made the biggest impression on him at the time was Julián Basílico Coco. Not that they kept each other's company; Coco was six years older and that seems like half a century to a teenager. Statius Muller would only meet him as an adult, but Julian only lived a few houses down the street in the working-class district of Colón, and even before he became widely known, he was legendary in the alleyways of Otrobanda.

One evening, the little black boy was sitting on the seawall down by the piers, playing proudly on his mandolin. The violinist Jossy van der Linde staggered by, drunk as a skunk. "Play the 'mi' on that thing!" Julián could not do it. "If you can't even do something as simple as that, how dare you call yourself a guitar player?" Julián was furious.

The subsequent guitarist and bassist would attend the Amsterdam conservatory after the war and play together with violinist Yehudi Menuhin, guitarist Andrés Segovia, and jazz trumpeters Stan Kenton and Dizzy Gillespie. At the beginning of the 1950s he would make several recordings with local musicians in the studios of Thomas Henriques or of Horacio Hoyer, a sound fanatic who would later found Radio Hoyer and record hundreds of 78 rpm records.

When Wim Statius Muller saw him rushing around Otrobanda, Julián was not even twenty and completely obsessed with music. At four o'clock in the morning he went into the Palm house because he had to solve a musical problem right away. Or he jumped up during a performance and shouted at the interpreter: "*Bo ta mierde! Bo sa?*" (You're full of shit! What do you think you're doing?) He would be referring to a surprising harmonic turn of phrase or some risky change from 6/8 to 5/8 time in the tumba.

Coco composed his first tumbas and boleros during the war and recorded them in Horoacio Hoyer's studio immediately following it. He adhered closely to the Cuban music tradition while at the same time gaining experience with European classical music by playing contrabass with the Curaçaoan Philharmonic Orchestra. Coco was also one of those men who lived in two or even three worlds.

"We were all obsessed with music," Wim Statius Muller told me. "But Julián took the cake. He spoke very softly, except when he talked about music. He changed into an apostle who shut the devil's mouth."

In 1943 a songbook called *Cancionero Papiamento* appeared, compiled by Julio Perrenal, a contraction of the names of Pierre Lauffer, Jules de Palm, and René de Rooy. Statius Muller remembers this too: the poets Lauffer, De Rooy, and De Palm, all in their twenties at the time, produced songs about daily life in wartime, about American GIs who stole the prettiest girls away from the local militiamen, about the curfew that brought with it a feeling of loss which had to be compensated in one way or another, about the scarcity of goods brought about by the blockade, and about the lively nightlife.

The plan to create *canticas* in their own local Creole was hatched, "half lying down, and half sitting, on a bench in the immediate vicinity of the graveyard, with the gravestones bearing mute witness" (René de Rooy). The three of them choose as rhythms merengue, Antillean waltz, bolero, and rumba. During their premiere on the Curaçaoan radio, the guitar player was drunk and the other musicians conspicuous by their absence, so they had to sing *a cappella* versions. The result was not exactly conducive to making the three poets' compositions into instant hits. Still, two lyrics became very popular and in 1944 everyone on Curaçao could sing along to *Merengue Mericano* (American Merengue) or *Mi Pushi* (My Pussycat).

Thirty years later, Statius Muller cast his mind back to those bygone days with such fond memories that he decided to set six poems by Lauffer to music. The melodic, strongly rhythmic poetry was inextricably linked to his childhood in Otrobanda, where one heard singing or five, six, or seven instruments playing in every street.

Wim was an afterthought child; his father was fifty-two when he was born. He passed away thirteen years later, in 1943. Wim had just finished high school when his mother died. Barely an adult, he had to look after himself alone.

The first job to earn him a pretty penny was as assistant editor to the monthly magazine *De Passaat* (The Tradewind) published by Shell Curaçao. His successor was to be the young poet Tip Marugg. "A house organ like that was just to entertain people, a sop," Tip told me half a century later in one his seldom-given interviews. "I wrote all sorts of awful articles for it, on the most absurd subjects. I found it distasteful, but I needed the money since I came from a poor family."

Tip kept working for the magazine until he was forty-seven; Wim quit *De Passaat* after eleven months and in 1949 left for New York, where he took Coco Palm's advice and enrolled at the famous Julliard School of Music. In 1953 he got his diploma in solo piano, in 1954 his master's degree. He also took composition classes at Julliard.

It was here he made his acquaintance with European music from the Atlantic Ocean to the Ural Mountains, from the Baltic Sea to the Alps. As a pianist, his mentor was Josef Raieff, the last exponent of Russian music at Julliard. The man who had been born in Charkov had lived most of his childhood in Chicago, but in the words of Statius Muller he remained "an authentic Russian." He was both amiable and demanding, a drill sergeant when it came to technique and a melancholic when it came to trying to sweep his students away to the profoundest depths of the musical soul. Raieff was trained by the Russian pianist Josef Lhévinne, who in turn was a protégé of the Russian pianist and composer Anton Rubinstein. Furthermore, Raieff had studied with Alexander Siloti, a student of Franz Liszt, and with Arthur Schnabel and Edward Steuermann. Schnabel was an exponent of the Viennese school and Steurmann of the German. Raieff was a one-man embodiment of practically all schools and streams of European approaches to performance. However, his preference was for the flowing Russian style, something that can still be heard in the velvet touch of Statius Muller.

Julliard was a home for European exiles. Josef Lhévinne's ghost still haunted the place, as did that of his widow Rosina, a Russian Jewish pianist. Statius Muller had just entered America, in the pink of health, positivist, open-minded, and in a certain sense still unspoiled, when he became Assistant Professor of Music at Ohio State University in Columbus.

He performed several times as concert pianist in Ohio and New York. Yet in the long run, life in Columbus did not appeal to him. Campus life was too secluded, too predictable, too monotonous. In 1960 he returned to Curaçao with his wife and two children.

He took a civil servant's day job. In the evening he sat behind the piano, notating with unprecedented speed the melodies that came to him with such apparent ease.

He had already written his first pieces for piano in the early fifties—well, not exactly written. In 1951 Horacio Hoyer took him into the studio, put a microphone in front of him and said: "Play something." There was not a single note in front of him and he began improvising on the spot. Six waltzes appeared on 78 rpm records. Only later would he began composing in a "harmonically richer" way, even though melodies would continue to occur to him "as metaphors."

In half a century Statius Muller composed one hundred and twenty Antillean waltzes, dances, mazurkas, and tumbas—and rumbas and calypsos, the rhythms of the former Spanish and English islands. After first editions on Curaçao, he was easily able to publish the dances with the New York music publisher the International Music Company. The Paris conservatory included his waltzes as part of its mandatory curriculum owing to the high level of pianistic prowess necessary to play them. I have never heard a single note of his on Dutch radio, though they are regularly played on France Musique.

Wim Statius Muller is the embodiment of a century of Antillean music. His works contain all its influences, techniques, and achievements. They are refined, rhythmically perfect, and deliciously melancholic in melodic terms. His only real competitor as a composer in the second half of the twentieth century was the pianist who used to live near him as a boy, Robert Rojer.

Rojer was nine years younger. Just before he left for the United States, Wim said goodbye to his piano teacher Jacobo Palm. "We're going across the street first," said Coco. "Robbie hasn't gone to bed yet, so you can still play something for him. He would really love it." For the nine-year-old Robbie it was a truly a big deal. Eleven years later Statius Muller returned to Curaçao. One evening he turned on the radio, tuned in to Curom, the Curaçao Broadcasting company, and heard a performance of Chopin's First Scherzo. It was brilliantly played, with a clear vision of how to perform it. A full-fledged talent. And then the announcer said: "You have been listening to Robbie Rojer."

Rojer had furthered his education in Holland, three years after Statius Muller had left. His music teacher at his high school in Eindhoven, Mr. Van Wouw, also gave lessons at the Royal Conservatory in The Hague. He helped Rojer cram to prepare for the conservatory's entrance exam, which he passed with flying colors at age eighteen. Rojer went on to study medicine and resumed his piano studies at the conservatory. His double career soon took on astonishing proportions. He opened a doctor's practice for the poor in Otrobanda, became a specialist as internist, wrote his dissertation, took his doctoral degree, practiced medicine in the Saint Elizabeth Hospital in Willemstad, was appointed professor at the University of Groningen, wrote three studies that measured Chopin's influence on Antillean dance music with the precision of a seismograph, gave concerts, and composed. You might well ask how it was all possible; the answer lay in Rojer's virtually perfect memory. An article he published fifteen years earlier in some scientific journal was something he could call to mind word for word; he could remember every single note of sheet music that had ever been in front of him on his piano.

Rojer (b. 1939) wrote ingenious music, with a flawless feeling for the various Antillean rhythms. He freed the Curaçaoan waltz from its diatonic simplicity and raised it to a high level of harmonic complexity. Apart from Chopin, Ravel is also an unmistakable source of Rojer's inspiration.

Statius Muller's music is more accessible than Rojer's, but conversely Rojer's music is more daring. He experimented with rhythms, continually pushing the envelope to explore new boundaries, and wrote quite a few waltzes for two pianos. The pianos complement each other, go their own separate ways, reinforce one another, or make a head-on collision. Rojer often plays the waltzes together with Statius Muller, and then they take on the aspect of a dispute. The composers are each other's polar opposites; Statius Muller's music seduces, Rojer's surprises. They react to each other, realizing all too well they cannot do without the other.

For Rojer, that dispute takes on an extra dimension. His grandfather Jacobo Palm, whom he calls "Pappa" like all the grandchildren did (in the family there is no distinction made between the father, grandfather, or great-grandfather), had given Statius Muller his first piano lessons. The respect Rojer harbors for Shon Coco Palm goes beyond honor and verges on devotion. And so he must always sigh when he says to Statius Muller: "Your waltzes are just as melodious as Pappa's."

23

My Sister the Negress

Wim Statius Muller's great-great-grandfather was Frisian, an East Frisian from the north of Germany who was called to become Lutheran minister of Willemstad. He would no doubt have been horrified at the thought of his great-great-grandson having dashed off a tumba at the age of eight. But for Wim's parents it was no longer a horrifying thought. They loved dancing the tumba and were overjoyed at their son having composed one. The tumba was a huge hit at home and naturally Wim had to play it for Shon Coco Palm. His piano teacher took a blank sheet of notation paper, wrote down the notes, and scribbled "Opus 1" in the top right margin.

Wim spent all his childhood vacations in the family's country home in San Sebastiaan, some twenty kilometers from the city, on the road to Westpunt by way of Sint Willibrordus. I drove past it scores of times, a white country building that looked more like a farmhouse in a country estate. Wim's father was not rich; he was a civil servant. A year after Wim was born his father quit his job because a young man who had just graduated with a law degree had come from Holland and taken the position originally intended for him. He was fifty-three at the time and out of desperation he began occupying himself with the family's country house. He imported three cows and a bull and let the pedigreed dairy cattle graze in the wild fields. There were 215 hectares of land surrounding the house, which ever since the abolition of slavery had no value whatsoever. Uncle Etie, Wim's brother, bought the former plantations of Veeris, Santa Cruz, Siberie, Fontein, and Bei Kas for a song, and from Cola Debrot's father he also purchased Ascención in 1925. Cola had spent three years there working on his novel *My Sister the Negress*, which for the most part was set in the horribly rundown Ascención estate.

On the grounds of San Sebastiaan were six small houses, lived in by plantation workers. The walls were made of clay, the roofs from dried stalks of corn. Because of their roofs the houses were called *kas di pal'i maishi*, house with a thatched roof of cornstalks. Wim was like family to the people who lived there. That is probably where he heard tumba for the first time.

Of his days at San Sebastiaan he still remembers the *seú*—feasts, the harvest celebrations. A procession was held at the end of the rainy season after gathering the corn and picking the peanuts and wild beans, accompanied with song and dance that wended its way to the church at Sint Willibrordus.

He did not get to hear the tambú as a white boy from the city. White men often went in secret to watch and listen to tambú, though they did not usually take part in dancing. "To be really able to enjoy it in peace you have to go to the outer districts," he told me, "to the plantations or the villages of Sint Willibrordus, Barber, and Boca San Michiel."

For Curaçaoans it comes as no surprise that Cola Debrot's novel *My Sister the Negress*, not the first full-fledged novel in Dutch Antillean literature in which the relationship between whites and blacks is examined, was situated in the outlying districts. Only in the yards of the country estates did white and black children play together like brothers and sisters.

The racial, social, and economic divide that existed on Curaçao remained intact until long after the abolition of slavery. The distance between the black and white populations of the island was greater than that between the island and the South American continent. Historically, it often resulted in bloody confrontations, ranging from disturbances where one or two people were killed to a veritable battle that only the police and army could put down. Twenty-six people were killed in the 1750 revolt at the Hato plantation. After the failure of the rebellion, an unknown number of rebels jumped to their deaths from the cliffs into the sea and thirty-four other slaves were sentenced to death. In the slave rebellion of 1795, which began at the Knip plantation and broke out all over the entire western part of the island, twenty-nine died.

In 1993, when I wanted to attend the anniversary of the 1795 slave revolt at Knip plantation house, I was refused entrance. I had just come to live on the island and had settled at Lagun, not four kilometers from Knip; I wanted to hear the speech given by Frank Martinus Arion, the author of the best selling book *Double Play,* a novel that reads like a musical score—the four main characters play dominoes throughout the book in a kind of *quatre-mains.* Near the entrance to the porch, I was asked in a friendly way to please leave the plantation. One of the organizers informed me that I was not dressed in a manner befitting the solemn occasion. I was familiar with the black population's dislike of short pants, Bermuda shorts, and t-shirts; I had put on a dark pair of trousers and a white shirt, the sort of clothes Curaçaoan men wore at funerals and other ceremonies. So what were they nagging about? There was nothing wrong with the way I was dressed. Then one of the organizers pointed to the collar of my shirt. "No tie." I was politely shown the door. I did not belong there, as the only white man among the two hundred blacks in attendance, with or without a tie, to come and commemorate the most heroic page in their history. I then realized that I was not going to have an easy time on the island—in any case, it would be a lot harder than the time I had spent in West Africa.

At first, it was not easy to come into contact with the ancestors of the earliest white settlers either. Islanders are mistrustful, and as far as that is concerned it does not matter whether you are staying on Curaçao, Corsica, or Martha's Vineyard. In the beginning, the only contacts I had were the poet Carel de Haseth and his wife Chila; but thanks to them I was introduced to Dudi Smeets-Muskus, and she in turn introduced me to several old Curaçaoan families. It would take another five years before I was invited to visit black families at home. I could drop in on the writer Tip Marugg at any time, but not on Frank Martinus Arion. I only made his acquaintance at a literary festival in Aruba, or, as Arion put it with a wry smile, "on neutral terrain."

All the same, Curaçao never turned into Haiti or Jamaica, where violence was first perpetrated against the whites, then the colored population, and, in the end, against everyone. In terms of language and music Curaçaoans have found a way to live in a certain kind of harmony, though not always with understanding. Blacks, Jews, white colonists, Venezuelan immigrants, and the Portuguese who came to Curaçao from Madeira after the construction of the refinery all speak Papiamentu. It is the language of everyone on Curaçao, Aruba, and Bonaire and has an important role to play in fashioning a sense of identity in a similar way to the Antillean waltzes, dances, mazurkas, and tumbas. Whenever a waltz is played at a party, blacks, coloreds, and whites all head for the dance floor and it does not matter whether you are of Jewish, Dutch, German, Swedish, Portuguese, or Venezuelan origin.

In other areas, the divide has continued to exist. It was quite exceptional that Statius Muller was able to attend a voodoo mass in a cave along the Hato plains. A friend of his who was an internist at the Saint Elizabeth Hospital led him inside. An evil spirit was to be exorcised from a young girl. She had spent two days in a dark cage before being led into the cave, dressed as a bride. Two extremely plump and scantily clad women accompanied her. They danced in front of an altar, and kept on dancing around the girl in circles. An hour later, the mass began, with several melismas sung by the Haitian priest Silesio. Statius Muller perked up. He could barely stand the atmosphere in the cave—the scared-to-death fourteen-year-old girl who had been let out of her cage like an animal constantly being sprayed with rum by the dancing women, who spit liquor at her . . . the screaming and moaning . . . the presence of two police inspectors there to make sure the mass did not descend into collective delirium. But the singing enchanted him.

Pope Gregory the Great clamped down on the use of melisma. The hallelujah was the only part of liturgical singing that was allowed to be ornamented. In every other case, he prescribed syllabic singing. Roman Catholics at the time switched over to using the rigid Gregorian chant, while the Greek Catholic Ambrosian chant continued to make ample use of melisma. How this way of singing ever got to Haiti and later on to Curaçao remains a mystery to Statius Muller. After all, the slaves were converted to Christianity by Roman Catholic missionaries. Since the Coptic Christians continued using melisma in their religious rites, he suspects that there must have been a shipment of slaves from East Africa to the Antilles, or via slave routes in the Sahara.

In any case, it was abundantly clear to Statius Muller that the music culture in the Antilles was much richer than is generally assumed. And, as with a great deal of music, it came directly from a religion.

On Curaçao, all you have to do is simply walk past any church to agree with this notion. The mass at six-thirty in the evening is attended by so many churchgoers that latecomers have to stand near the entrance doors. All the windows and doors stay open, which makes it possible to hear the choir every evening. It sounds like a thousand voices singing, in choirs that swing, singing Antillean church songs that sound like American Negro spirituals.

Whenever I went to buy fresh bread in the nearest supermarket, I always lingered for a moment near the church, swaying to the music. I took all the variations on themes to be spontaneous improvisations, to be pure jazz. But they were melismas.

24

Spy

In the late twentieth century, the majority of Antillean dances were composed by musicians who lived and worked in Europe, because they were homesick. Once again they mirrored Chopin, who had written most of his mazurkas in Paris, and Manuel de Falla, who composed his *Siete canciones populares españolas* during his seven-year residency in France.

When there were only thirty thousand inhabitants on Curaçao, the island was pretty much self-sufficient. The population increased fivefold after the Shell refinery was built, and practically all food-stuffs had to be imported from Venezuela and the United States. Prices skyrocketed. Composers and musicians could scarcely make a living from live performances and giving lessons, and took day jobs. Johnny Kleinmoedig took his degree in notarial law and put it into practice, reading deeds during the day. He had completed his studies in Leiden and it was there that he felt "different" for the first time in his life, "with a different outlook on life and a different set of manners." Robert Rojer commuted back and forth between the Netherlands and Curaçao; in Willemstad he operated on patients, and in Groningen he taught medicine at the local university. Livio Hermans took his degree in Amsterdam in pharmacology and a degree in medicine in Louvain in Belgium. He subsequently shuttled back and forth from Curaçao to Aruba and Bonaire as part of his several jobs in the health care system and was often on a plane bound for Europe.

Wim Statius Muller figured he could spend the rest of his life behind a piano once he got his degree from the Julliard School of Music. In 1960 he was given a teaching position at the Pablo Casals Conservatory in San Juan, Puerto Rico. He had already packed his bags when the Puerto Rican parliament decided to slash the conservatory's budget. Statius Muller had to stay on Curaçao and take the first job that came his way, at the Government Public Information Service.

Two years later he switched over to the newly set up Antillean Intelligence Service. From 1968 to 1972 he was head of the AVP—precisely at the time when Curaçao was undergoing social and political revolution.

In May 1969 Shell fired several hundred workers. The black workers were told that they could do the same work for a subcontractor with a ten to twenty percent cut in salary. That was asking for trouble. Or begging for a revolt.

The contract between Shell and the subcontractor had been signed, sealed, and delivered. The unions demanded it be reviewed, so negotiations could be resumed. At first the government stood by and watched before finally giving in to the union demands, and put pressure on Shell. On the morning of May 30, it looked as though headway were being made, but in the meantime thousands of demonstrators were marching to the city center. Before the parties took their places at the negotiation table, parts of Willemstad were already in flames.

Ignorance and incompetence went hand in hand during those days in May. Politicians blundered; the authorities woke up too late. Naturally, that is not the way Statius Muller put it. For him Curaçao "was confronted with the release of social tensions which the establishment had seriously underestimated." Because the government dragged its feet, the pro-government union leaders lost all authority over their members. At first, the only support for the strikers came from the Algemene Haven Unie (General Harbor Union). Fearful of losing membership, all the unions radicalized their positions. The conflict led to a massive demonstration that, owing to ineffective police action, ended up in rioting, plundering, and arson. A labor conflict that had gotten out of hand led to a political revolution.

Trinta di Mei, as it is known in Papiamentu, resulted in four dead, a scorched gap in the heart of Otrobanda, and a deep mistrust between sections of the population. Statius Muller felt those disastrous events could have been prevented, "but the revolution was inevitable, if not then, then certainly later." The black population was fed up with colonial rule.

The governor under whom Statius Muller served in those days was Cola Debrot. Put another way: the composer served under a novelist. In 1969 Debrot was coming to the end of his term as governor. When the riots broke out he was in Puerto Rico, on his way to New York. Deeply shocked, he returned immediately to Curaçao. As governor, he had no direct political influence; he was merely a representative of the Dutch head of state. The only thing he could do was try and calm the situation.

That was no easy task after the thirtieth of May. Practically all white politicians had to leave the arena; a young generation of black politicians took their place. It was a total revolution. When Debrot received the four leaders of the revolt at the government house, the white segment of the population washed their hands of him forever.

Debrot had been a constant champion of the process of creolization in all his novels, stories, poems, and essays: irrespective of the color of one's skin, the same Creole heart beat in every Antillean breast. Cola had spent the first years of his life in Bonaire at the plantation house at Slaagbaai. Just like Statius Muller, he was a native son, a white Creole, who harbored endless sympathy towards the black population. When The Hague urged military invention, he sent back a telegram in code: "Forgive me if I aim before I fire." He had studied medicine and law in the Netherlands, been included in the ranks of the literary group around the magazine *Forum*, and was friends with the prominent Dutch authors Du Perron and Ter Braak, as well as the painters Pyke Koch and Carel Willink. Debrot had worked for the World Health Organization in Geneva, where he had become friends with a great author-to-be: Louis-Ferdinand Céline, who at the time was still just Mr. Destouches. Cola Debrot was as European as one would imagine judging by his last name, but for an intimate and candid conversation he chose to speak Papiamentu, the language he had learned from his father and his *jaja*, the black nanny who raised him a child.

Towards the end of 1969 he felt a tad lonelier with each day that passed. Statius Muller remembers Debrot called him often to invite him over to Government House for a glass of sherry. After a string of questions about the current situation, a gloomy Debrot changed the topic of conversation to the future. He then talked about music, which put him at ease. Debrot was knowledgeable and quite a connoisseur of music. Statius Muller: "It was no coincidence he was married to a ballerina."

He left office in February 1970. At his farewell reception, black, white, and brown were all conspicuous by their absence. From universally respected intellectual he had been denigrated to *person non grata*. Debrot spent the last years of his life in Laren, the Netherlands, at the Rosa Spierhuis, a senior citizen's home for artists.

The much younger Statius Muller left two years later for the Netherlands, where he went to work for the BVD (the Dutch Intelligence service). He did such a good job that NATO offered him a position, first in Rome and later in Brussels, where he became an executive officer of the NATO Security Office. He retired in 1995.

When working for Dutch intelligence, he had to keep a low profile. He performed every now and again for a small circle or during vacations on his native island, but whenever he was invited to play on radio or television, his superiors always advised him to politely decline. In the left-wing 1970s, it was a national sport to literally throw stones in the agency's backyard, and anyone working for it did well to project the image of a bland civil servant. At the time, the weeklies had a field day, publishing hilarious features about how the agency kept tabs on aged communists, anarchists, and pacifists or followed the coming and goings of the radical student movement. Statius Muller had nothing to do with this; his job was to chart terrorist cells. For many, that was just as idiotic as it was despicable; members of the left-wing press, myself included, were afraid of a witch-hunt against squatters and Maoists who only adopted the rhetoric of the Red Brigades and the Red Army Faction and had the lethal capacity of a cap gun.

But the BVD was not just chasing after phantoms, as proved by both the fatal shooting between RAF members and the Utrecht police, in which one victim died, and the occupation of the French embassy in The Hague by Japanese terrorists. It was sometimes better to prevent worse things from happening by taking action at the last minute, but that was not something the BVD wanted to shout from the rooftops. It was a thankless job: blunders made the papers, while successful actions went straight into the archives as top secret national security files. Statius Muller led an isolated existence and could only share his homesickness for the Antilles with his Curaçaoan wife Sally Führing. It was during this period that he composed his most wistful pieces of music.

The spy who dismantled terrorist cells during the day, composed amiable Antillean waltzes in the evening. I had several conversations with Statius Muller and kidded him, calling him the James Bond of music. To him that was much too romantic a notion of what espionage was all about. Spying was nothing more than gathering as much information as possible. But it could not have been as dull as all that; the times that he talked about his work, I heard about infiltrations and meticulously planned actions that successfully prevented attacks. I could scarcely see the connection between these activities and the gentle musician who, moreover, had a phenomenal knowledge of Antillean and European classical music.

Composer/security officer. Not without a trace of pride did Statius Muller inform me during our conversations that he was the second composer who had engaged in such activity. Liszt had gone before him. He was a spy for the Prussians in the salons of Paris during the Franco-Prussian War. But he had not been much more than an informant. That was not the case with Statius Muller, who had been a spider in a web of intelligence.

Statius Muller would have liked nothing better than to live safely within the confines of a conservatory. Had he been born in a large country, that would have been possible; at age thirty he was regarded as highly talented and at age forty as an accomplished composer. But it was his lot as an islander to have to find a job.

In one sense, his time as an intelligence agent had been inspirational: composing was his ideal form of release. Perhaps he would have composed less had he had another line of work. But he lived a double life—at home he was someone else. At home at the piano, he became "the man I had always wanted to be."

25

Fifteen Hundred Out-of-tune Pianos

The Dutch heard all sorts of things in the Antilles, but nothing special when it came to music. In 1990 the correspondence between Chris J. Engels and J. van der Walle was published. The former had gone to Curaçao in 1936 as a missionary doctor and became a pivotal figure in its cultural life. In 1940 he started the literary magazine *De Stoep*, which included works by Cola Debrot and Boeli van Leeuwen and the literary debuts of poets Tip Marugg and Frank Martinus Arion. He founded the Curaçao Museum, organized the first Van Gogh exhibition in the Western Hemisphere, and placed a sheet steel statue by Marino Marini (which would later be sent to the Guggenheim Museum in New York) in front of his lovely renovated country estate house. His wife Lucilia, daughter of the musician and composer Rudolf Boskaljon, shocked the world with her cubist paintings of tambú dancers. Johan van der Walle was editor in chief of the Curaçao newspaper *Beurs-en Nieuwsberichten*, correspondent for the Dutch press agency Aneta, and author of five novels, all of which were set in the West Indies. The correspondence between Engels and van der Walle looked back over fifty years of literature, visual arts, and politics. In a subordinate clause, Engels writes of the "pleasant little waltzes by the Palms" which he heard on a festive occasion—a phrase that sounded as stuck-up as it was condescending.

Engels should have known better. He was an extraordinarily gifted musician who could hold his own with any professional pianist and regularly performed Mozart piano concertos with the Curaçao Philharmonic Orchestra. He even tried his hand at composing and considered his variations on the theme of the Dutch children's song *Hup Marianneke* as one of his finest works. He demanded that every Dutch pianist perform that work on Curaçao, or else their trip to the West Indies would not take place and the invitation from his father-in-law Boskaljon would be withdrawn. Engels acted like some kind of cultural pope, and that would not have been such a mortal sin had he propagated the work of other Dutch Antillean composers with as much fervor.

The funny thing was that most of the composers—in any case all the Palms—were Doctor Engels's patients. Whenever they felt under the weather or were sick he visited them in the late afternoon, after he had finished his daily one-hour session of fencing. Like some errant knight in his snow-white fencing outfit, visor still on his head and foil in hand, he stepped out of his Austin Minor, just as out of place amid all the big American gas guzzlers. He would not hear of receiving any payment; instead, in exchange for a medical consultation he asked the musicians for a handwritten composition. His turned out to be a sizeable collection of musical scores and it is still in the Stroomzigt estate, which remains property of the Engels family; to this day, the collection has not even been studied, let alone catalogued.

The only time Johan van der Walle mentions music is in his memoirs of Aruba. The island only became a tourist resort after World War II. Before the war, the only foreigners to frequent the island came from the United States to run the oil refinery or from Venezuela to do business. The wide beaches were completely unspoiled at the time. Van der Walle mused about the Aruban "hour of the donkey," the first hour of the afternoon when everything turned silent and the air above the beach shimmered with heat. He would sink into a deep sleep, from which he would only awaken toward sunset, when the blood-red sun sank into the ocean.

He describes Oranjestad as a sleepy little town with weird and wonderful houses built in an inimitable, flamboyant style. They did not have the stately import of the old houses of Curaçao, which especially in the countryside took on the demeanor of forts. Building on Aruba had only taken place after the forts built on the coasts of Ghana and Guinea were no longer in use, and their counterparts in Curaçao, Puerto Rico, and Cuba had begun falling into disrepair.

The soil on Aruba was too infertile to start plantations; it made no sense to bring any slaves to the island. In the first half of the nineteenth century the Aruban countryside was uninhabited and the only ones to spend any time in the barren land were the political refugees from Venezuela, who sat around their campfires singing melancholic songs. Echoes of these songs could be heard in the music of the Aruban Padú Lampe and Dadaatje, the Aruban chanteuse who sang songs based on the Venezuelan joropo.

Dadaatje had been ravaged by a terrible disease at a young age. She was confined to a wheelchair, the legs lovingly tucked in each day by her husband Tom, Padú Lampe's brother. She listened dreamily to her brother-in-law's piano playing or that of Rufo Inocencio Wever, who had lost his left arm in a traffic accident and played the melody with his right hand while tapping away at the keys with his wooden left arm in a staccato style.

Before the war there were fifteen hundred pianos on Aruba. Nevertheless, it was not even possible for the piano tuner who had come from Santo Domingo to earn a living, because the Arubans were much better at interpreting their intimate songs on untuned instruments than on tuned ones.

Aruba, in the recollections of Van der Walle, was a haven for "lively artistic people." He also came to the conclusion that the island was much more South American than Curaçao. I don't know if this is true; islanders go to great lengths to find features to distinguish themselves from each another. As proof of Aruba's South American character, reference is often made to a 1935 performance of the Argentinean tango singer Carlos Gardel. Accompanied by three Argentine guitarists, he sang in Oranjestad and the next evening in San Nicolaas, a sinister town a stone's throw from the oil refinery. When I visited the town in 1997, the air was still practically unbreathable. In the local café-theater—which looked more like a brothel—Gardel sang his last notes. The next day he travelled to Colombia and the plane crashed just before landing in Medellín. Arubans like to brag that Gardel had left the island with the applause still ringing in his ears—he had to give three encores and left the stage with ladies fainting all around him. They forget that on May 24, 1935, just before his departure for Aruba, Gardel had performed on Curaçao, on the 25th for the second time, and the 26th for the third day in a row.

Aruba has a different history from Curaçao and less tradition. For centuries the island had been a sleepy place of little consequence that only awoke in the era of rapid transportation and worldwide communications. Arubans adapt more quickly than Curaçaoans; they do not resist foreign influences as much, adapting them to fit their own lifestyle. They gloss over cultural differences more easily; there is less hate and envy on Aruba. Arubans are proud of what they have achieved, and rightly so. It has become a well-to-do island, much more prosperous than its immediate neighbors, but Arubans are not so concerned about keeping up a distinct sense of identity.

Juan Chabaya Lampe, nicknamed Padú, grew into a phenomenon on the piano. He released ten long-play albums in Venezuela, and in the postwar years you could hear him at least once a day on Radio Caracas or Radio Maracaibo, though four or five times was more like it. He played in Colombia, Puerto Rico, Santo Domingo, and, in the 1950s, in Hotel Nacional in Havana, the same hotel where Frank Sinatra performed. The rich Americans who heard him there invited him to come and play in Miami, New York, or Seattle.

The piano playing of Padú, who in the meantime took to calling himself Padú del Caribe, went the same way as the island of Aruba itself. It was immensely popular with American tourists and rapidly veered towards showbiz entertainment. At its best it really swung, which is why such jazz musicians as Randal Corsen, Eric Calmes, and Izaline Calister often referred to Padú. At its worst, it sounded a little too slick.

But on Curaçao I heard another Padú, the way he used to be; and certainly when he played *quatre-mains* with his daughter Vivian and started to improvise, you could hear all those fifteen hundred pianos on Aruba playing.

26

Music Everywhere

Just before I left for Curaçao, a slight panic came over me. I had just spent several months on Dominica, and the only music that filled the streets of Roseau had been reggae. I could dream the songs of Bob Marley.

I had packed my record collection in twenty boxes and stored them in a warehouse with all my other personal belongings. The high humidity in the tropics would only warp them; it seemed senseless to take them with me. As the moving man was taking away the boxes I asked myself what I was going to do without Bach, Mozart, Schubert, Shostakovich, Debussy . . .

A week before leaving, I started making tapes as fast as I could. It was a race against the clock; I should have gotten started a lot earlier, but hey, when you are leaving for several years there are quite a few things that need doing. In the end I sent two boxes by overseas surface mail.

I could have saved myself the effort. You can hear any kind of music you want on Curaçao. There are fourteen radio stations on the island that broadcast Antillean, Venezuelan, Colombian, Dominican, and Puerto Rican music twenty-four hours a day. On Saturday and Sunday you can listen to old Cuban *son* and boleros on three different stations. The national radio station broadcasts classical European music every afternoon from one to two P.M. to usher in the siesta. You can listen to classical music on the other stations every evening of the week.

On my first Good Friday on the island, five different stations broadcast the complete *St Matthew's Passion*. I chose the first one on the dial, a Polish rendition from the 1950s. It was exceptionally beautiful, and again made me wonder why Antilleans were so charmed by a country that had never had any relations with the tropics.

Totally in keeping with Chopin, who showed the deepest respect for Bach, I heard partitas, fugues, and toccatas performed on Curaçao. It always reminded me of my meeting with Gabriel García Marquez. To him, the Netherlands belonged to Curaçao, not the other way around. Recalling the visits he had made to the island with his grandfather, he had told me with great decisiveness: "For us Colombians, Europa began on the quays of Willemstad."

In the evening on Good Friday, the *St Matthew's Passion* was performed in the basilica of Pietermaai, just like it was in Dutch cities. The choir and orchestra were made up of amateurs who had been rehearsing since the searing heat of November. The traditional Christmas concert takes place in another church; you are not considered a real islander if you fail to attend that concert. The choir reflects the make-up of the population; the whites are principally descendants of the two thousand Portuguese who made the journey in 1920 from Madeira to Curaçao to work at the oil refinery. Their *fado* voices mesh beautifully with the deep basses of the black singers.

At least once a month there is a recital given on the island by a foreign soloist. A reputable band performs every month on the outside patio of the plantation house Brievengat, and every month five to ten thousand spectators flock to the festival stadium for a musical happening that lasts all night.

What surprised me most about Curaçao was how much people knew about music. Nowhere else in the world had I met so many music fanatics as on Curaçao. It did not matter which kind of music, either; the annual jazz festival attracted as many visitors as the annual tumba festival or performances by Colombian or Caribbean bands.

Doctor Efraim Cijntje let me hear the percussion instruments the slaves had made. Cijntje, the son of a black Surinamer, was a psychiatrist working at the Capriles clinic. He walked around during the day in a white jacket, but in the evenings he trained himself playing drums, musical saws, and other idiophones. He became a much sought-after percussionist. As he showed me, slaves had made instruments out of all sorts of materials, from iron cylinders with which they grated maize, or from saws and hammers. Sometimes the instruments imitated the instruments of the last remaining Indians. The *wiri* descended from the scraper that Indians in Mexico, Colombia, and Venezuela had used to accompany their ritual dances. The *manga* (an iron pipe), the *barbá* (an iron armband), and the *chapi* (a spade or hoe head) are real slave instruments. The *kalbas den tobo*, the big calabash water drum, is also a beloved instrument of the Senoufo and Malinké, peoples who live along the border areas of Ivory Coast, Burkina Faso, Mali, and Guinea. To reduce the size of the sound box, three-quarters of the calabash is filled with water.

Erwin Prudencia collected all those percussion instruments for his CD *Transishon*. Prudencia wanted nothing to do with the semi-European music until he found the waltz his father Emilo had written for his mother in the 1950s. Of course the waltz was named after his mother. He duly recorded *Virginia* in a version for guitar and wiri.

I met Frank Davelaar, high school music teacher, tenor and choir leader in his spare time. He translated *Peter and the Wolf* into Papiamentu and conducted the performance himself. I have never met a man more knowledgeable about music. He has seen practically every opera there ever was, all over the world. Finally there was one left he had not seen, *Les Troyens* by Hector Berlioz, a long, large-scale, and thereby hugely expensive opera that was seldom staged. Sometime in the 1970s the opera had been programmed in New York. He faked having a cold, played hooky from school and flew to New York on a Friday, via Aruba. There had been a delay in his connecting flight and he had to give his New York taxi driver a big tip to step on it and exceed the speed limit to get him there on time to hear the opening strains of *Les Troyens*. He flew back to Curaçao on Sunday night, and on Monday he was back in front of his pupils, with trembling hands. Not because of jet lag, but because of what he had heard: a choir that had shaken the very walls of Lincoln Center.

In many ways, Dutch Antilleans are sectarian, except when it comes to music. Then they make no distinction between Caribbean, colonial, African, classical, or pop music. Their only criterion is whether it is good or bad, and that dividing line runs through all sorts of music.

The time Frank Davelaar came to visit me, it took quite a while before he actually reached my yard. He had lingered on the gravel path to listen to the steel pan music my black neighbor was playing on his old gramophone. He owned quite a few 78 rpms recorded in the 1940s, during the oil refinery heyday—Antillean waltzes, played on steel drums.

27

Chick Corea

I moved yet again, this time to a house in the Penstraat. It was next door to the Vianen plantation house, which at the beginning of the twentieth century had been the last house in the city. Right behind it had been the mangrove swamp of Marie Pompoen. The plantation house, built in 1815, was in a deplorable state; I did not quite understand why, since everywhere else in the city the plantation houses had been renovated or transformed into office buildings, restaurants, or supermarkets.

For as long as people could remember, no one had lived at Vianen. After I had rented the little cottage next door, I found out the reason why. Long ago Vianen's owner had fallen from an outside staircase. He had broken his neck. Fine, that had been an accident. But when the daughter of the next owner also fell from the staircase, people on the island figured the house must be haunted. Incidentally, the girl survived the fall because she fell into the rain barrel. But the third time would not be so lucky, and the third inhabitant of Vianen would meet a horrible end. And so there never was a third inhabitant.

My cottage, which had once been a part of the plantation and had been the residence of the overseer, was situated right on the waterfront. It was sheltered by a wild almond tree. It was small, quite small, not thirty square meters; the porch outside was twice as large. A tiled roof provided shade for the porch; two side walls kept out the wind. The entire front of the building was open.

From the porch I had a panoramic view of the ocean and the entrance to the harbor. I had breakfast in the company of frigate birds, pelicans, dolphins who leapt out of the water, and ships bound for the harbor. Later I asked myself how on earth I had been able to work there; it was a place to stretch your legs and stare constantly at the horizon. The best place on earth, that is, whenever I was there.

When I was not, the thieves struck, and after the twentieth break-in I decided to leave.

One morning I saw a passenger ship moored close to shore. It was still there the next day. A beautiful vessel, I estimated it must have been built somewhere between 1950 and 1960. It was white, and blue just above the waterline, with twin funnels, both also painted dark blue. The ship was called *Freewinds*. It lay for a week in front of my window before entering the harbor and mooring along the Handelskade.

During the European winter, two or three cruise ships put into Curaçao on a daily basis. When the European summer starts, the entire fleet crosses the Atlantic and plies the waters of the Mediterranean. The ships return to the Caribbean in October.

They all look a lot like each other. I did not notice right away that the *Freewinds* had anchored in the harbor. When it was still there the next month, Curaçaoans began asking themselves why it had not sailed out to sea, on its way to its next destination. The harbor authorities let it be known it was undergoing renovations, and indeed the island's finest carpenters went to work on the interior. Money did not seem to be an object; the finest wood was brought on board. Two months later, painters hung on ropes along the ship's hull; four months later, the ship looked as good as new. It was then made known the ship was owned by the Church of Scientology.

Curaçao remained the home port for the *Freewinds*. Every other week the ship set sail for a seven-day cruise; then it lay for another week in the harbor. The passengers were rich and often American celebrities, movie stars, ad agency bosses, producers, TV stars, or artists, all members of the Church of Scientology. They took courses on board, and, exhausted from the bright lights of the media circus, they came to their senses. Nosy islanders were kept at bay; it was impossible to get close to the ship, let alone come onboard. The secrecy started to get irritating.

One evening, Chick Corea performed on deck. To dispel the islanders' suspicion, it was decided to let a limited number of visitors attend the concert. I knew Chick Corea to be a passionate jazz pianist with wide-ranging interests. In the Netherlands I had bought an album of his on which he played two Mozart piano concertos with the *Wiener Philharmoniker* (Vienna Philharmonic). He approached the music differently from classically trained pianists, refreshingly more like improvisations on old themes.

I bought a ticket for the concert so I could also see the insides of the ship. It turned out to be money well spent; I had never seen such opulence in my life as I saw onboard the *Freewinds*—that is, in the section I was allowed to enter. Security guards closed off the dining hall and the cabins; I could not set foot outside the three corridors that led from the central hall to the lounge, where the concert was to be held.

I estimated there to be about two hundred Curaçaoans among the audience. There was less interest among the ship's passengers: no more than fifty came to hear the concert.

Chick Corea came on stage, sat down in front of the piano, and apologized to the audience. He had planned to perform a number of his best-known pieces, as had been indicated on the program notes. A walk through the city had made him change his mind. In a café in Otrobanda he had heard local music being played, the tumba. The next day he had gone back to the café, this time staying some four hours, requesting one song after another. He had taken notes, about the rhythm, about the melodies. Once back on the ship he had gone to the piano and started improvising, based on his notes. He wanted to play the results for us.

He was taking a big risk doing this. In the audience were several black Curaçaoans who had taken in the tumba with their mother's milk, and about ten musicians.

"Am I playing it right?" he asked after the second improvisation.

"Perfectly," replied one of the local musicians. "Except for the last jump in the measure."

"Can you show me?"

The man stood up and tapped out the rhythm on the framework of the grand piano.

What came next were three new improvisations, each between twenty to thirty minutes long. And every time Corea crowed out loud: "This rhythm is unique; this rhythm is one of a kind."

People from small countries crave approval. Whenever they get it from a celebrity from a big country, they dispense with being modest and beam with pride from ear to ear. That is what happened that night as well; the local musicians left the ship standing ten feet tall.

Chick Corea was not just any old musician, and he had given the tumba his blessing. Unique: that was what the islanders wanted to hear.

The number called *Tumba Island* appeared on his next recording. Chick would go on to play it many many times, with several variations, at concert after concert. In fact, he was joining the ranks of a long tradition that had begun in the nineteenth century. Just like his fellow countryman Gottschalk, he had had a fling at Caribbean music. He was following in the footsteps of Louis Moureau, of Scott Joplin, of Gershwin, and of Harry Belafonte and the Andrew Sisters. In the mid-twentieth century they had picked up on calypso, and calypso had made them world famous.

28

Dirty Jim/Mighty Bomber

The Mighty Bomber was a gentleman. Blue suit, white shirt, red tie. He lived in Laventille, one of the most dangerous neighborhoods in Port of Spain, Trinidad. He had nothing to fear himself, since even in the pitch dark of night the people of Laventille bowed deeply for the elderly singer.

At one time he had whipped crowds into a frenzy with his throbbing voice, but sitting across from him now he spoke more softly than a priest in a confessional box. Just as he did with every other visitor, he told me about the heyday of calypso, about 1941, 1942, 1943, when singers ranted and raved against the American soldiers based on the island.

Talking with the Mighty Bomber, I discovered quite a few similarities between Trinidad and Curaçao. Every European power had left its own distinctive mark on its colonies in the West Indies, but nevertheless, despite the visible differences in terms of architecture and styles of living, the islands of the Greater and Lesser Antilles have a great deal in common.

Calypso, which became popular on Trinidad, developed along the same lines as the Curaçaoan, Cuban, and Puerto Rican danza. Its origin was partially European.

In 1783 the Spanish tried to develop Trinidad by luring French planters who had had much experience growing sugar cane on other Caribbean islands. The amount of land they were allocated depended on the number of slaves they brought with them, and they did not have to pay a single cent for it. Quite a few Frenchman took up the offer. They took their own music with them, and at the end of the eighteenth century that would have been the minuet. Mixed with *bèlè* dance performed by the slaves, this resulted in calypso. The difference between the bèlè and Curaçaoan tambú is negligible: the rhythm is beat out on the drum; the singer asks questions, the choir gives answers. Tambú and bèlè share the same strong narrative element. The minuet was slipped underneath the narrative.

Was it really that simple?

In my travel book *De regenvogel* (The Rainbird), I describe the rituals and songs of the tribes that lived deep in the jungles of Gabon. Two years after my book was published, the CD *Lambarena* was released. Two French nationals, Mariella Bertheas and Hugues de Courson, and one Gabonese, Pierre Akendengue, came up with the idea of combining the traditional songs of the peoples in the jungle with the music of Bach. The two forms of musical expression came together in Lambarena, the village where Dr. Albert Schweitzer had built a hospital. Every evening Schweitzer used to play pieces by Bach on his piano with organ pedals in his house situated next door to the hospital; he was a gifted organist who financed his hospital by playing concerts all over Europe. According to the CD's compilers, Schweitzer bridged the gap between the different cultures; that is not quite the truth. Albert Schweitzer looked down on the indigenous culture and had no interest in it whatsoever; he was more like Boskaljon, who wanted to propagate European culture.

To the French and Gabonese, Lambarena was mainly a geographic crossroads: at one time you could hear both the vibraphone and *Herr, Unser Hersscher*. In the jungle the CD compilers made field recordings of the traditional songs of the Fang people accompanied by drumming and then mixed it with Bach fugues, preludes, cantatas, or segments of his *St. John Passion*. The result is surprising. The Fang songs keep to the same rhythm as the choirs from the *Passion* and elapse along the same melody lines. Mind you, the compilers did not tamper with Bach, like some jazz pianist occasionally does by performing a fugue with more swing, nor did they tamper with the traditional songs; all they did was combine the two recordings to let us hear that German church music and African ritual songs are based on the same musical principles. The combination makes Bach more rhythmic and the Fang songs more melodious, and the only conclusion you can reach is that both kinds of music are a perfect fit.

Just as perfect as the *bèlè* and calypso.

The French planters did not just bring their music to Trinidad; they also introduced carnival in the mid-nineteenth century. At first it was celebrated only by the whites. When the lower social classes took it over in the twentieth century, the upper classes withdrew. Carnival turned into a popular festival with—in the eyes of the whites—a rebellious and vulgar character. Prior to the grand procession, a festival was organized to select the best calypso of the year. Curaçao adopted this tradition with its annual tumba festival.

The sounds of protest could be discerned in both the lyrics and names of the calypso singers. Mighty Bomber, Relator, Lord Superior, Mighty Terror, Attila the Hun, and the Roaring Lion whipped audiences into a frenzy by addressing social evils in their performances. Texts were improvised on the spot. One singer after another took his turn and the audience chose the winner of the verbal wars by singing the refrain: "I beat you, you're dead."

In 1920 work began on an oil refinery on Trinidad. In order to refine the huge reserves of Venezuelan oil, the oil companies made deals with one another: Shell would set up shop in Cuba, Standard Oil in Aruba, Shell in Curaçao, Standard Oil in Trinidad. And so it came to pass; the Shell refinery in Havana was an exact replica of the one in Willemstad, the Standard Oil refinery on Aruba was exactly the same as the one in Trinidad. At the end of 1941 American military forces were stationed on all four islands to protect the refineries from German U-boat attacks. Prostitution flourished in the immediate vicinity of the army barracks. Alcohol abuse assumed catastrophic proportions and infected the local population. These were the years of rum and Coca-Cola.

The Curaçaoan chronicler Jules de Palm described these years with good-natured humor. "After February 1942 downtown Willemstad was dominated by the American soldiers who had come to protect us. They were both literally and figuratively received with open arms, much to the chagrin of the young men on Curaçao, who had sadly discovered that their supposedly irresistible charms had been reduced to zero. The girls would not even give our own militia men the time of day; they saw in every uniformed American a Robert Taylor or a Clark Gable. The officers were press-ganged by the local society clubs and introduced to their marriageable daughters, who responded eagerly to their advances."

But the Curaçaoan poet Pierre Lauffer did not see any humor in it. He wrote about the "shameless brutes who have carved out such swathes of pain on my land." And the Calypsonians of Trinidad spewed fire.

After the war, not all the Americans left. On Curaçao one of them began to organize evenings with tambú dances for the cruise ship tourists. On Trinidad an American soldier transformed a former rum factory into a calypso club. He gave it the name Dirty Jim, to commemorate the legendary 1930s calypsonian of the same name. Dirty Jim's Swizzle Club was frequented by both black and white customers.

Calypso flourished in the postwar years like never before. It gained international stature through Harry Belafonte, whose mother came from Jamaica and father from Martinique. In the 1950s he recorded four albums with calypsos, selling more than a million copies of the hits *Matilda* and *Banana Boat Song*. The Andrew Sisters made an old calypso song world famous with an expurgated version of "Rum and Coca-Cola"—in the original version, by Lord Invader, the American soldiers are filthy good-for-nothing pimps who lure girls and their mothers into prostitution in pursuit of the almighty dollar.

The Andrew Sisters sang it fantastically. It was ironic, biting, provocative.

In the 1950s all Antilleans danced the calypso and, even for classically trained pianists like Wim Statius Muller, the calypso was a perfectly logical choice of rhythm. Statius Muller wrote two pieces that blended it with the tumba, calling them tumba-calypsos. By this time nobody realized the calypso had descended from the minuet.

In terms of music, the Antilles were a laboratory. Long before the terms *fusion* and *crossover* entered the music vocabulary, people on the islands had already been experimenting for years.

For the Mighty Bomber, the thing that characterized the essence of Caribbean music was that it had developed through resistance to the powers that be: against French, Spanish, English, and in the end, American domination. When Trinidad gained its independence in 1962, the enemy disappeared. "It was," in the words of the Mighty Bomber, "good for us and bad for the music." Calypso was demoted to a mere form of entertainment.

On Curaçao, Ellis Juliana and René Rosalia reached the same conclusion. The spontaneous tambú disappeared, and commercial forms of music had taken its place. Tambú singers began making money doing performances and, by using the microphone, they overwhelmed the audience during the traditional call and response sessions.

It had once been exciting to perform tambú. In the weeks immediately preceding the New Year, the tambú singers and dancers moved around the island like lightning. Whenever the police headed toward the sound, the musicians hopped on the back of a flatbed pickup truck and drove off. A couple of kilometers down the road they would start another tambú. They crisscrossed the island in this way; *tambú nervioso* was a form of sport, just as boisterous as a game of dominoes, though more of a challenge, since dominoes had not been banned.

29

Mazurka Erotika

In 1993 the *Antilliaanse Luchtvaartmaatschaapij* (ALM) reopened a direct flight from Willemstad to Havana after more than thirty years, thus re-establishing economic and cultural ties between Curaçao and Cuba.

Schooners had once plied the waters between the two islands, maintaining a regular link between Havana and Willemstad, then cargo and mail boats with only a few cabins for passengers, and from 1904, passenger ships. Just after the turn of twentieth century there was a shortage of work on Curaçao. No less than half of the male working-age population embarked for Cuba in third-class cabins or as deck passengers to cut sugar cane on Cuban plantations. It was seasonal work; some of them sailed back home, most stayed in Cuba for years and only came back to Curaçao when they could find work at the oil refinery that had just been built around the Schottegat. They took back with them the *tres* guitar, *marimbula*, and bongos, and they played *son*.

In the 1950s most Curaçaoans listened to Radio Havana on Saturdays and Sundays. The influence was huge; suddenly all the dance bands had a brass section. Bands such as Sexteto Gressman, Conjunto Cristal, and Estrellas del Caribe blared away to their hearts' content, leaning heavily on Cuban styles of playing.

A new generation of musicians came to the fore, among which Boy Dap (b. 1933) and Oswin "Chin" Behilia (b. 1938) are the most famous. Chin Behilia combined Cuban son with tumba and added a narrative element. His numbers are true ballads, narrative poems about everyday life or the hope of the common man to win first prize in the lottery. Chin often called in the assistance of Julian B. Coco, the guitarist who had made such a deep impression on Wim Statius Muller. Together they made warm music, part Curaçaoan, part

Cuban. Singing and telling a story were one and the same for Chin; all of Curaçao stayed home on Sundays to watch his weekly television program *Telepatria* in the 1980s. After telling a story he grabbed the guitar and just kept on, with his melodious voice resounding just as high and clear as Ibrahim Ferrer.

Going the other way around, the Aruban pianist Padú Lampe took the tumba to Cuba. He got standing ovations when he played at the Hotel Nacional on the seafront boulevard in Havana.

The exchange that had lasted decades came to an end when the United States instituted its trade embargo against Cuba in 1962. The revolution that Fidel Castro and Che Guevara unleashed on Cuba did not get much support in Curaçao. The black population found the revolutionary leaders too white, while the whites abhorred Communism. Not a single ship docked at Willemstad harbor from Havana nor set sail bound for it. The newly founded ALM airline's only northbound route was for Miami.

The revolt in 1969 did little to change the situation. To be sure, the demonstrators chanted slogans during the march on Otrobanda that could have come straight from Castro and Guevara's repertoire, but the radical leaders were more sympathetic to the Black Panthers and Malcolm X than they were toward the Cuban revolutionaries.

The generations that grew up in the 1970s and 1980s had nothing in common with Cuban music. Reggae took the place of *son*, and salsa and merengue began their victory march throughout the Caribbean.

I flew to Havana in January 1994. The ALM had offered such a favorable package deal I was able to stay in a majestic room in the Hotel Nacional for a pittance. Cuba was in the throes of a crisis. Since the breakup of the Soviet Union, Cuba could no longer count on Russian assistance. Gasoline had been rationed; practically all public transport had ground to a halt. Actually getting a chicken leg in a restaurant at the time was considered nothing short of a miracle.

But I heard music everywhere. A different ensemble played in every restaurant and on each floor: two guitarists and a singer, or a guitarist, a trumpet player, and a singer, or two old men who stood next to your table rendering a son or bolero. One of the men told me that the son had originated in the region where he had been born and that it had been derived from the French minuet. Five years later, I would recognize the man in Wim Wenders's documentary film *Buena Vista Social Club*: Ibrahim Ferrer. Watching it in the movie theatre, I was also suddenly confronted with the pianist Ruben González, who I had heard playing in another restaurant, a somewhat more upscale establishment in a formerly fashionable neighborhood in Havana. The *Buena Vista Social Club* film and CD would make Cuban music world famous, but in 1994, Ferrer and González were two nameless old men trying to make a few bucks playing in restaurants in the evenings.

For those musicians, practically nothing had changed since the nineteenth century. Even then, pianists and composers kept friendly company, trying to help each other out if they possibly could. They were dreamers, outside of society. In his book on Cuban music, the writer Alejo Carpentier portrays the composer Nicolás Ruiz Espadero (1832–1890), an Erik Satie *avant la lettre*, who lived in his mother's house for forty years, surrounded by cats, sheets of music paper, and a piano. His moustache hung below his chin and whenever he turned his head to one side, the end hung above his shoulder. He only ventured outside once in a great while, and then only in the evening, and then only to inspect a piano that had just been offloaded from a ship. Espadero performed in public only twice: once solo and once with Louis Moreau Gottschalk. Carpentier wrote: "His existence was one long romantic dream, with panoramic views that had precious little to do with the reality outside his own window."

Cuban musicians kept out of political debate, had nothing to do with a succession of dictators or racial separation (in the mid-nineteenth century they collected money for José White, so this black violinist could further his music studies in Paris). Reading about their history brings just as much of a tear to the eye as does watching González and Ferrer in Wim Wenders's film: old men who can hardly believe they are playing in New York. All of a sudden they were popular, all over the world.

Countless Cuban orchestras flew to Curaçao with the ALM. In May 1994 the first Cubans came to perform when Lionel Capriles, director of Maduro & Curiel's Bank, turned sixty. He invited friend and foe, shareholders, and the entire bank personnel for an evening buffet in the Sonesta Hotel. Thousands of Curaçaoans went to the party. The night sky was studded with stars when the fifteen-man orchestra took the stage that had been especially erected on the beach. It would be a phenomenal performance, the high point of which was the bank director's dance with the three Cuban female vocalists on stage in the spotlights. Lionel Capriles moved effortlessly to the music, performing a kind of tambú. Capriles? Yes sir, he is a cousin of David Capriles, who as a member of the Colonial Council had once banned that *tambour* dance.

It must have been about a year later when the Cuban jazz pianist Gonzalo Rubalcaba came to Curaçao. He improvised on Cuban rhythms with such dexterity his hands turned into flashes of lightning. Rubalcaba not only popularized Latin jazz, but also the practice of improvising on local dance rhythms. Jazz improvisations of the tumba and danza were soon heard on Curaçao.

In 2001 Izaline Calister won the tumba festival with her song that praised the Otrobanda district. She has a brilliant voice, high, husky, swinging, agile; she has such personality you immediately associate her with carnival and the Caribbean style of living; she performs barefooted and lets the usually rattling sound of Papiamentu flow smoothly by, singing the consonants softly, like it is done in Cape Verde and Brazil.

Calister is a model for the young generation of Dutch Antillean musicians. She finished her conservatory studies in the Dutch city of Groningen, in the jazz department. She met Randal Corsen, who asked her to sing two songs for him as part of his final exam for his conservatory education in Tilburg. A year later it was the other way around: she asked Randal to accompany her on piano for her own final exam. Together with bass player Eric Calmes, they laid the foundation for a band; Calmes had studied at the Amsterdam conservatory.

Calister, Corsen, and Calmes had all heard the same thing from their respective families: "Take a leaf out of professor Robert Rojer's book, study, get a degree, and do music as a hobby, for the fun of it." Randal Corsen allowed himself to be persuaded. He enrolled in a Polytechnic Institute in Eindhoven, in the architecture department. After a wasted year ("my buildings would have fallen down"), he took the entrance exam to the conservatory. Izaline did, however, take her master's degree in business administration at Groningen University. Her parents could now be satisfied, but when doing an internship for a company, she enrolled in the conservatory. The thought of having to go to an office every day gave her "the creeps."

For Corsen, Calister, and Calmes, taking risks was part of the deal. Maybe they would end up like the Cuban Espadero, with only forty cats to their names, or end up famous in old age like Rubén González and Ibrahim Ferrer. But Esapadero, González, and Ferrer had made a living out of music all their lives and the young musicians wanted to follow their example.

The three of them wrote songs together. Calister wrote the lyrics and sometimes the beginning of a melody. Calmes and Corsen made the arrangements. Their band incorporated the use of the *wiri, agan, kachú, beku, chapi, marimbula, tambú grandi,* and other Curaçaoan percussion instruments. Their music is much more African than compositions by the Palms, but what they do share with their musical forbears is taking the rhythm of the waltz, mazurka, danza, and tumba as starting points.

By far, the loveliest song that Izaline Calister and Eric Calmes wrote is a mazurka. "*Ku bo boka na mi boka,*" are the opening lyrics to their *Mazurka erotika*: "*ku bo aliento den mi orea / ku bo mannan na mi kurpa / nos pashon ta kresa den nos kursason*" (With your mouth on my mouth, your breath in my ear, and your hand on my body, passion grows in our hearts).

When you hear Izaline sing those words, you cannot do anything else but acknowledge that the mazurka, born in the snows of Poland, only thawed out completely under the Antillean sun.

30

The Tumba Queen

I asked Izaline whether it was the dream of every Curaçaoan girl to become Tumba Queen. She could not say if it was. Her mother had sung, her stepmother had sung, her older sister, her brother. For her, singing just came naturally.

When she was seven she joined Rudy Plaate's children's choir. They rehearsed every Sunday afternoon from four to seven at Uncle Rudy's and Aunt Emmy's, on the porch, outdoors, around the piano, under the roofed-in patio. There was always food, there was always fruit juice; in between songs she feasted on mango pie. Every Sunday was a party.

The twenty-five-piece choir sang two- or three-part harmony to words put to a waltz, mazurka, danza, merengue, ranchera, or tumba Plaate had written. Without being aware of it, she was getting a thorough grounding in the classic forms of Caribbean music.

She rehearsed for recordings or the Christmas show on television. Rudy Plaate's choir was just as much a part of growing up on Curaçao as school bags dangling from shoulders, school uniforms, knee socks, and yellow school buses. Every child could sing along with *Perlitas*, the little pearls.

Over the years Izaline learned to sing hundreds of songs. She knows them all by heart, word for word.

At home she listened to Richard Simon's *Misa Alegre*, the Joyful Mass, which indeed was so exuberant she immediately wanted to go to church. One of the highest voices in the choir was her stepmother's. Or she listened to the folk songs Plaate recorded and released in the 1970s. The beautiful full voice in the choir was her own mother's. The recordings were an audible memory, and the only concrete thing she had to remember her by, for her mother had died of a cerebral hemorrhage when Izaline was three.

Five years later her father remarried. Her stepmother loved singing and was in a choir; they hit it off immediately. Ever since then she refers to "my own mother" and "my mother."

Izaline's father had to fight to make something of himself. He came from a simple family, growing up in the working-class neighborhood of Montaña. He graduated from high school and won one of five scholarships to further his studies in Holland. Back on the island he designed houses for the rent-control housing corporation Fundashon Kas Popular, later specializing in the restoration of historic buildings. Her stepmother began as a teacher at a domestic science school, worked her way up to becoming its director, and gave Papiamentu lessons at the Pedagogical Academy. Her parents moved into a house in the well-to-do Jongbloed neighborhood, an achievement they reached through their own efforts. They wanted the same for their children. So get an education. Stop bellyaching, and get good grades.

Izaline continued her studies in Groningen. She never missed a class and enjoyed the life of a student, being unattached and enjoying the freedom that was total compared to her childhood on the island. She never wanted to leave Holland ever again.

She did not get homesick until later, and then it was not because of a lack of good weather, but because she missed her family after having been away for five years. She came from a close-knit family and her brothers and sisters had grown up sharing everything. Most Curaçaoan families are not complete, but when they are, the kids stick together like glue. And it is always open house in the Antilles; all day long aunts and uncles, nephews and nieces drop by for a chat and a drink. Doors are never locked and shutters are only closed to keep out direct sunlight.

In Groningen, for a good time she went to the city's bars or "brown cafes," as they are called, where she sang in a succession of local bands. Everyone kept telling her she had a great voice and ought to go to the conservatory. She did not consider it for a second; she was chronically insecure about her singing talents.

She finished her course in business administration and went to work as intern for a company. It turned out to be an island in miniature—an office space in which everyone watched what you were doing all the time. In a fit of distress she telephoned the conservatory.

She would just be able to take the entrance exam; official registration had already closed. There was no time to prepare, for two days later she had to do an audition.

Years later the conservatory director confessed to her: "Technically, it was a disaster, but I thought: this woman's got something." He gave her the benefit of the doubt.

The first year was horrible. She knew nothing about jazz, little about classical, and nothing about pop music. No, she had never heard of the Stones; she came from another world. All she knew were boleros ("start tapping out a bolero and I can sing it") and Curaçaoan waltzes, something at which the conservatory turned up its nose. She had the breathing skills of a person struggling to swim ashore so as not to drown, she had bad timing, and could not read a note. All criticism was personal—at the university a D meant you had not learned the subject well; at the conservatory it meant that you could not sing well.

The color of her skin caused the most confusion. People expected a black female vocalist to have a dark full voice like Mahalia Jackson: hers was high and light.

For a year she fought against the academic conception of music. Yet in the end, she gave in: technique is a part of singing. Outside the conservatory she took singing lessons in classical music. Solfège, reading music, singing scales, timing. She practiced singing Italian arias—she could not bring herself to sing the German ones because of her horrible accent. She had no problems with Italian; every Sunday morning her father had listened to operas by Donizetti, Bellini, Rossini, Verdi, and Puccini.

The second year was better. But she felt small, very small. Eric Calmes helped her get over her doubts. He was an Antillean, lived in Amsterdam, taught at the Rotterdam Conservatory; he came to Groningen talking sense to her all night long. "Hey, why are you making things hard for yourself? You are twisting yourself into all kinds of contortions to sing in English or Brazilian Portuguese. Sing in your own language!"

She followed his advice. Not that she got rid of her feelings of uncertainty; she suffered a week of sleepless nights before every performance. But when the moment arrived, she overcame her fear.

Eric Calmes introduced her to Randal Corsen and proposed that she write her own lyrics. She dared taking the step to Papiamentu and wrote the lyrics to *Mazurka erotika*.

A year after graduating she formed a ten-piece band with Eric Calmes, Randal Corsen, the renowned percussionist Pernell Saturnino, and her younger brother Roël, a beginning drummer. A bit like a business administration graduate would do it, she drafted the concept for her first album neatly typed onto a single sheet of paper.

The starting point was to be *muzik di zumbi*, the music of the spirits that was played on the *benta*, a special instrument of African origin. It consists of a bowed branch of a hardwood tree strung with fiber from a coconut. One of the ends of the bow is held to the mouth in such a way that the oral cavity acts as a resonator. To produce the thin sound, the fiber is made to vibrate and the pitch is altered by enlarging and reducing the size of the oral cavity and by moving the tongue.

She wanted to combine the music that is played during the *seú* feast, the annual harvest celebration, with the *benta*. On Palm Sunday the *seú* groups make their way—singing and dancing—to the village of Barber. The women wear traditional costumes: white blouse, white dress, around which several multi-colored swathes of madras cloth are draped, and a headdress, also of madras. The men dress in a white shirt and wind a broad, brightly colored cloth around their hips, over their black trousers. Percussion instruments accompany the singing, so her CD must be based on percussion. The rhythms the seú groups perform are the waltz, the danzón, and the contradance. The instrumental accompaniment is limited: it consists of little more than a *cuarta* and a flute.

That is precisely what she wanted on the CD: lots of percussion instruments and just a piano and bass guitar, which would add elements of jazz to the traditional *muzik di zumbi*.

The voices were to alternate with one another. In the seú songs the soloists tell of the abundant harvest that has just been taken in, while the choir sings the praises of the feats achieved. The harvest festival celebrates sweetness, both the beauty of *Dushi Kòrsou* (Sweet Curaçao), the epithet which the islanders themselves use to describe their homeland, and the solidarity among its people. To follow in the footsteps of tradition she decided to close the album with *Fiesta di piskadó*, a popular song her teacher Rudy Plaate had composed in the 1960s. The first line reads: *"Nos a ba'fo'i nos boto ku no kurason yen di alegría"* (We leave our boat with our hearts full of joy). It is a fisherman's song; the catch has been successful and now all the villagers can sing and dance.

They recorded the CD in a studio that turned out to be much too small. Eric Calmes said: "By recording in a space that is too small, we kill our own music." She went into debt, took out a mortgage on everything she owned. A big studio cost a thousand euros a day. After ten days of recording and ten days of mixing she had spent 20,000 euros and she still had to pay the first small studio.

She departed for Curaçao with two suitcases stuffed with CDs. She practically fainted when she landed at the airport. If the customs officer asked her to open her bags, she would have to pay import duties on every one of the CDs hidden under her thin summer dresses. She said a quick little prayer and looked down bashfully. "Anything to declare?" "No." "Really?" "No." She was allowed to pass through.

After giving a few radio interviews she played at Froots—an open-air restaurant. To her "surprise" there were some eight hundred people there on folding chairs. The first night she sold four hundred CDs; the second night Gibi Doran offered to write a tumba for her, so she could compete in the tumba festival. Doran led one the island's most popular bands.

She was up for it. Not to win, just for the experience. The tumba festival had been a part of her childhood, of her culture. She just wanted to take part for once in her life, singing with a twenty-piece band in front of an audience of ten thousand.

Amidst total bedlam she sang "Much'i Otrobanda." For the first time in a long time, the audience heard an unadulterated tumba, and not one of those *roadfire* numbers that had blown over from Trinidad, as had been the case in previous years—a Curaçaoan tumba, sung by a barefooted vocalist. That too was a huge hit; women performers had become scarce at the tumba festival. For the past decade only men had taken the prize.

Her going barefoot led to all kinds of speculations. Was it a homage to the Cape Verdean singer Cesaria Evora? To the female plantation slaves? Or to *Perlitas*, who rehearsed on the porch? She had to explain it to the throng of journalists. "Very simple, I can't sing with my shoes on."

Barefoot, she hit the front pages of every newspaper: E REINA IZALINE (THE QUEEN IZALINE).

She won and the whole island went hysterical. She thought it was a little scary—Dutch Antilleans never go crazy. Women all wanted to throw their arms around her in a motherly embrace, men wanted to kiss her full on the mouth, children wanted to touch her, everybody started grabbing at her. During carnival she was surrounded by seven bodyguards.

The run-up to carnival lasts fours weeks: one *jump-up* after another, from nine in the morning until late at night. She performed at every school, place of business, bank branch, office, or government building, without a monitor or microphone. It had a disastrous effect on her vocal cords. Now she was performing in a parking lot, now right in the middle of the street. After Curaçao came Bonaire; the entire band went to the neighboring island on a chartered flight twice. There too she performed at every school and every office. After a quick trip to Aruba, it was finally time for the grand finale on Curaçao. Every radio station wanted her in front of a microphone, every TV station wanted her in front of a camera in the studio or outside on location. She crisscrossed the island visiting every neighborhood and village.

Carnival itself consists of three parades: the grand procession during the day, the children's parade in the dark on Tuesday evening, And the *gran marcha,* which lasts eight hours. The *Reina di Tumba* ensconced on the most lavishly decorated float is expected to sing her song when passing by, otherwise the audience gets angry. Thirty, forty, fifty, sixty times she sang "Much'i Otrobanda," with only a ten-minute break.

I saw Izaline come past, as I walked alongside the float, in the Penstraat where I was living. The black ladies living across the street, the old men in the wooden house next door, the rastas in the house on the corner, the daughters of the Portuguese shopkeeper, all my neighbors agreed that Izaline was the most beautiful, wittiest, exuberant, sweetest, and most talented *Reina di Tumba* that Curaçao had ever had.

Not a word of it was untrue. She swayed back and forth, barefoot, down the streets, bowing to each and every spectator. White, black, brown, Asian Caribbeans, Jewish businessmen, even slightly grinning *makambas*, everyone fell in love with Izaline. Even the sound of her name was melodic, and once you heard it, you would never forget it. She was just as captivating in person; she did not put on airs, she stayed herself, a nice girl who was delighted to be a one-time queen of the island. As queen, she even became a self-appointed reconciler between rich and poor.

Curaçao had great need of such a unifying figure in the first years of the twenty-first century. Economically, things were going downhill; the poor neighborhoods were turning into slums, crime increased so quickly practically every citizen carried some sort of weapon. A survey indicated that some thirty thousand households had a gun at home; the atmosphere turned grim. Carnival was supposed to do away with these kinds of troubles in a rush of glamor and glitter. Izaline once again brought together the wasted-looking welfare cases who had to get by on 220 Antillean guilders a month, the tough street kids with their hot gold necklaces and Rolex watches ill-gotten through armed robberies, and those people practically too afraid to leave their houses. Even the Haitians, the fastest growing group of illegal aliens, asked her to come and sing for them among the shacks they had built from the ruins of houses and the containers in which they cooked and slept.

Her mother followed her around every day with cups of fruit and vegetable juice, her boyfriend from the Dutch province of Drenthe with jars of honey. It came to no avail; first her vocal cords became swollen, then she felt lumps in her throat. She had had to sing too often, and too loudly. And she had to continually be on her toes.

When a Tumba Queen is not looking, someone drapes a mantle around her shoulders, with a company logo on it. The cameras flash and the next day she is in the papers like some kind of mannequin in a store window. Carnival is pure entertainment for the participants; the groups who have worked hard month after month to make the best-looking float all make an altruistic effort. But rampant commercialism lurks behind the scenes.

Politicians also want to cash in on carnival. Every party tried to get into her good graces. Wouldn't she like to come down to party headquarters to receive a medal! Again, for a photo-op in the newspaper or to flash a big smile on the TV news. She sent her mother instead, only hesitating once when the party dedicated to doing away with corruption and nepotism asked her to become an honorary member. She was sympathetic toward the innovators who had decided to search their own consciences and build a future with a new élan. In the end, she asked her mother to do the honors, so as not to spoil the illusion. You are Tumba Queen for everyone, not for a certain party or segment of the population.

It took her two years to get over her chronic exhaustion. Back in the Netherlands, her ear, nose, and throat specialist identified serious swelling of the vocal cords and advised her to take it very easy with her voice for a while, otherwise she would be chronically bothered by growths and her singing career would be over.

When she had finally recovered from carnival, she made a new CD with traditional numbers, to the disappointment to her fans. She had had enough of pop music forms; she wanted to explore new territory. She called the CD *Mariposa* (Butterfly), after the 1895 danza of the same name by Joseph Sickman Corsen. Half a century later, a new arrangement had been made by Jacobo Palm that he provided with lyrics. He asked for the help of Yolanda and Charles Corsen, two of Joseph's grandchildren, both of whom were poets. However, it was the third grandchild, Camila, who put together the lyrics. She sat day after day in front of her piano, constantly repeating the words "*e mariposa, color di rosa,*" until she finally found a new set of rhymes to finish the lyrics. Yet another fifty years passed and Izaline asked Randal Corsen to arrange the danza for the third time. For that is what she intended to do: keep changing without losing sight of tradition.

She gave her third CD the symbolic title of *Krioyo* (Creole), a term mainly used in a culinary sense in Curaçao. The Dutch Creole kitchen mixes African influences (millet) with similarities to the American South (lots of deep-fat frying) and Dutch (no meal without cheese). She aimed to do the same with her music; she bases it on Afro-Caribbean rhythms without renouncing European influences. She can be inspired just as easily by *muzik di zumbi* as she is by the waltzes and dances by the Palms, Jacobo Conrad, Jo Corsen, Padú del Caribe, Wim Statius Muller, and Robert Rojer. But without innovation the classics become worn-out, empty shells and die out.

31

End of an Era

In 1999 Wim Statius Muller was asked to participate in the Chopin Memorial Concert in New York City's Lincoln Center. At the request of the organizers, he programmed one of his own compositions, the waltz *Nostalgia*. The participating pianists were introduced in turn by David Dubal, Billy Joel, and Tony Randall. Billy Joel's words about *Nostalgia* were: "This 'Nostalgia' says it all! It's what this evening is about."

Back on the island Wim told the anecdote with an appropriate sense of pride, although he was also slightly upset. Present and future had been done away with and he had been relegated to those who longed for the past.

Statius Muller realizes that he is indeed at the end of an era. The same holds true for Robert Rojer. They both play Chopin, Debussy, or Ravel with as much ease as they do works by Conrad or Blasini. They have carried on the tradition in which it is more and more difficult to extend the possibilities of the waltz, contradance, and mazurka. In Europe, art music had developed from tonal to atonal; in the Caribbean, composers remained faithful to tonality, even though Gerry Palm sometimes balanced on the edge. They experimented with the rhythm and could not go much further than to shift accents; after all, they were stuck with dance beats that form the essence of Antillean music.

Statius Muller and Rojer end the classical era. Their only heir is Johnny Kleinmoedig, who quite elegantly bid farewell, in the form of a couple of his own compositions, to Gerry, Coco, Dòdò, Albert, John, and Edgar Palm, to Jules Blasini and Jacobo Conrad, to Chris Ulder, Joseph Sickman Corsen, Paul Quirino de Lima, Emilio Naar, Charles Maduro, and Isaac De Costa Gomez. However,

Kleinmoedig has enjoyed the most success with his own ensemble that plays much closer to the folk music tradition.

Wim Statius Muller tried to modernize the Antillean waltz. At one of his first recitals in New York back in 1953 he played works by those considered the avant-garde of the day: Pijper, Voormolen, Badings, Strategier, Andriessen. Ever since, he asked himself how he could drag the Antillean waltz into the twentieth century. He explored the boundaries. Robert Rojer went even further—quite cleverly, in Statius Muller's opinion; if Ravel had lived on Curaçao he would have composed waltzes in the same vein as those by Rojer: "With Robbie the melody arises from the harmony, in my case harmony from the melody." But Statius Muller swore to me on numerous occasions: "the more I modernize, the less Curaçaoan my music becomes. The final destination is Ravel, Debussy. Spanish music is also governed by the same limits; there are also some dissonant chords in the works of Da Falla and Albeniz, but Spanish music must remain tonal, otherwise it ceases to be Spanish."

One foggy morning in Vienna, Statius Muller stepped into a music store, stamped the snow off his shoes and placed his order: a waltz by Schoenberg.

"Where are you from?"

"Curaçao!"

"And they know there that Schoenberg wrote a waltz?"

After searching for it a while, he handed him the score. "The last one I have left, and probably the only one left. Commissioned by the Vienna city council . . . Berg and Webern got the same commission to pay homage to their fellow townsman Johann Strauss."

"Extraordinary."

"Yes, you will be surprised. No matter how much the pioneers of atonality squirmed, they could not escape. To compose a waltz, they had to go back to tonality."

When Statius Muller began learning Schoenberg's waltz, he realized that he would never be able to extend the boundary. Not past a certain point, not past tonality. That is, not past Ravel, who had pushed it to the limits.

On Caribbean islands, music never lost contact with the people, and vice versa. Just like Spanish music, Antillean music is based on folklore. That is both its strength and weakness.

Every Curaçaoan, Bonairian, and Aruban knew the waltzes, dances, and mazurkas; they could whistle the tunes, hum or sing along with them. Arubans even chose one to be their national anthem, the swaying waltz *Aruba dushi terra,* composed by Rufo Wever and Padú Lampe, and at its public debut there was not a dry eye in the house.

Seductive, enticing: that is the essence of Antillean music. It could not push back frontiers; it was too rooted in old traditions. Having started with Chopin, after a long detour, it always came back to Chopin. To break out of this vicious circle, it had to seek refuge in jazz.

32

Bal Colonial

Composers from Martinique and Guadeloupe had come to a similar conclusion much earlier.

My first visit to the French Antilles was in 1989, four years before I had settled on Curaçao. At the time, I had nothing with which to compare it; what I had heard about music there all had to do with Saint-Pierre, the former capital city of Martinique.

On May 8, 1902, a Thursday and Ascension Day, Mont Pelée erupted and in less than two minutes wiped the city of Saint-Pierre at the foot of the volcano off the face of the map. There were only two survivors from its population of thirty thousand.

Throughout the nineteenth century Saint-Pierre had been a formidable rival to Havana, San Juan, Port-au-Prince, and Willemstad. It was beloved by travelers owing to its ambience and architecture, praised by opera singers, actors, and musicians because of its theater and numerous dance halls, praised by sailors for the celestial beauties in its brothels. A port city, it exhibited clear-cut similarities to the old quarters of New Orleans, an epicenter of music and entertainment. People used to say it was the liveliest city in all the Antilles, the most sinful city in the Antilles.

The gas that leaked from the volcano exploded with such force the shock could be felt in Bonaire and Trinidad.

In the nineties, I paid several visits from Curaçao to Martinique and Guadeloupe and paid greater attention to the differences between the French and Dutch Antilles.

The plantations on Martinique and Guadeloupe were not that large; they were much smaller than on Haiti, Cuba, Jamaica, or the outlying districts on Curaçao, where they could be as large as fourteen hundred hectares; the farmers there were *des petits blancs*. In the nineteenth century those farmers mixed with the freed slaves.

A century later no one on Martinique or Guadeloupe was all white or all black.

That mixing took place with the music as well. Just like on Cuba and Curaçao, the locals made European music their own. Waltzes, mazurkas, and polkas could all be heard on Martinique and Guadeloupe. But the connection to African rhythms came a lot sooner. The polka became the spicy *beguine*, and near the end of the nineteenth century it leaned toward New Orleans jazz.

The biggest difference between the Netherlands Antilles and the French was that the music of the French Antilles caught on in the motherland—in Paris. There was a historical reason for this; during the mass slaughter of World War I, France quickly went through its eligible soldiers and recruited thousands of young men from Africa and the West Indies. In 1918, they did not all go directly back home. Those who could play instruments found employment in Paris dance halls.

Antillean music became all the rage in the 1920s. Paris had at least five, six, or seven dance clubs where biguines, waltzes, and polkas were performed. They bore such names as Bal Colonial de la rue Blomet, Bal de la Glacière, La Cabane Bambou, La Boule Blanche, l'Elan Noir, La Savane, Madinina-Biguine. The veterans could not cope with demand and sought reinforcements from back home. Scores of musicians from Martinique and Guadeloupe set sail on ships bound for France. The poorest among them slept on the decks of cargo vessels of the Compagnie Générale Transatlantique or made the voyages as stowaways. In Paris, they took hotel jobs, usually as bellhops, and at night they played in the dance bands.

The arrival of Josephine Baker increased attention for black music. Baker gave her first Parisian performance in 1925 in the Théâtre des Champs-Elysées accompanied by a big jazz orchestra, the core of which was formed by Antillean musicians.

On Martinique and Guadeloupe itself, the music had already started leaning in the direction of jazz. In Paris this process could be further developed. The orchestras swung away with gusto. They played mazurkas in two parts, the first a fast one and the second slow, in such a way that it gave the dancers the opportunity of nestling against one another. They played waltzes, biguines, Cuban rumbas, cha chas, and habaneras.

In the same period, the Colonial Council of Curaçao banned the tambú. Any attempt to send an Antillean dance orchestra to Amsterdam would have been thwarted by the local authorities. The Palms never performed in the Netherlands, let alone a popular tambú singer or tumba orchestra.

In France, Antillean music did not limit itself to Parisian dance halls. The gramophone had scarcely been introduced to a mass market when the musicians found themselves being hauled into recording studios. In the 1920s and 1930s, they played on seven hundred sides of 78s.

I heard some of those old recordings on the double CD *Biguine, Valse et Mazurka Créoles*, that I bought in a little store in Fort-du-France. A mazurka such as *Souvenirs de Saint-Pierre* does not really differ in essence from its Curaçaoan counterpart, but it is performed in a totally different way. The clarinet plays the melody, the piano provides the accompaniment, reinforced by percussion instruments and the banjo, and presto, you practically have the sound of New Orleans jazz. The habanera called *Martinique* is strongly reminiscent of Curaçaoan Jules Blasini's contradances, but, despite that, sounds much more modern. The clarinet, guitar, and piano all take turns soloing, improvising on the theme, and you ask yourself whether the guitarist might not be Django Reinhardt himself. In Paris, the Antillean musicians were allowed to go even further.

The popular success of the dance bands from Martinique and Guadeloupe lasted until World War II. In April 1940 L'Exotique Jazz orchestra made its final recording, a languid waltz given the title of *Sur les flots aux Antilles*. After the war, bebop conquered the cellars on the Saint-Germain-des-Prés. The Antilleans, who in the meantime had become penniless old men, went back home, but they could pride themselves on having been the ones to make Paris ripe for jazz.

33

The Pilgrimage

The idea to attend the Chopin commemorative service in the Church of the Holy Cross of Warsaw and the three-day concert in Zelazowa Wola came from Dudi Smeets-Muskus. She took her mother with her, as well as the pianist Livio Hermans, Wim Statius Muller, and his wife Sally. In Poland they were joined by two Cubans, one Dominican, one Puerto Rican, one musician from Martinique, and one from Guadeloupe.

In the Polish snow, the Curaçaoans decided to do the commemorative service all over again, at home, with a Chopin marathon. Again Dudi organized the concert, and practically all the Antillean pianists took part.

I was staying in Munich at the time, and only heard about the concert when I got home. Naturally it had been a success, despite the excruciating heat, but those in attendance had experienced it as the end of a long era. Someone then raised the question of whether or not to do the same concert over again in 2049 and the answer of the majority of them was: no. Young Antillean musicians were increasingly bringing the African elements of their traditional music more to the fore than the European components. That tendency still holds true in the twenty-first century.

In that same year, 1999, a memorable evening took place two thousand kilometers to the north. At the invitation of the Polish-American Kosciuzko Institute, Wim Statius Muller played a number of Chopin's works in alternation with his own Antillean compositions at Alice Tully Hall in Lincoln Center in New York. Not only could he count on the greatest possible attention being paid, but he saw the audience's growing astonishment. Polish music being transformed into Caribbean music: this was a revelation to Polish Americans.

It was scant consolation; on the Dutch Antilles themselves, the waltz and mazurka seemed to have been relegated to oblivion. But then the opposite occurred.

It seemed as though every musician at the turn of the new century had turned to classical music. Randal Corsen recorded the works of his great-great-grandfather. Harold Martina released an entire album of works by the practically forgotten Curaçaoan composer Emirto de Lima, who had emigrated to Colombia. Freddy Arthur de Costa Goma—known to everyone as Tutti—found a pile of music scores by his grandfather, the composer Isaac Alfonso de Costa Gómez (1903–1958). Since Curaçao no longer had any suitable recording studios, he took a plane to Cuba, rented the Estudio Ojalá in Havana, and hired six Cuban musicians. He had his grandfather's music scores and those of Albert Palm (1903–1966) arranged by the pianist Paula Suárez. The same thing happened that had occurred when Randal Corsen had performed the pieces by Jo Corsen: after blowing off the dust, the music sounded as good as new.

When I arrived in Curaçao in the 1990s, there were scarcely any recordings of Antillean classical music to be found in music stores. The only album in stock was Harold Martina's collection of danzas. At musical evenings I often heard the waltz *Anna* by Albert Palm being performed, yet it did not appear on a single vinyl album or CD. On *Recuerdo Di Siglo 20* by Tutti da Costa Gómez there are three works by Alberto, the bass player among the Palm dynasty.

In 1999 the mezzo-soprano Tanja Kross won the incentive prize of the Rosa Ponselle International Competition for Vocal Arts in New York and in 2000 first prize at the Christina Deutekom Concours. The Amsterdam Concertgebouw Orchestra chose her as Rising Star of the 2004/2005 season; she gave a recital in its Kleine Zaal and went on a tour of the most important classical music venues in Paris, Salzburg, Vienna, Athens, Cologne, Birmingham, and New York. Curaçaoan Tanja had come to the Netherlands at the age of seventeen to study at Utrecht Conservatory. Nine years later she was giving a recital in Carnegie Hall, ten years later she was playing to full houses in the Staatoper Hannover in the role of Cherubino in *Le Nozze di Figaro*.

The best was yet to come. Universal Records offered her a contract, and she was allowed to choose the repertoire for her debut album. So what do you do? You look at Cecilia Bartoli, Nigel Kennedy, Janine Jansen—young, beautiful, talented singers whose careers have taken off like rockets—and you follow their example. You choose Vivaldi, a sure-fire success. But Kross, of Surinamese-Jewish-German-West Indian-Curaçaoan descent, chose works by Prudencia, Clemencia, Behilia, and Lecuona; by her fellow countryman Emilio Prudencia (1919–1974), who led a quiet life and composed a couple of gorgeous waltzes and danzas; by René Clemencia (b. 1957), one of the pioneers of Grupo Serenada, an ensemble dedicated to the rediscovery and preservation of Papiamentu song; by Oswin "Chin" Behilia (b. 1938), the Curaçaoan minstrel who blended Cuban son with native tumba; and by Ernesto Lecuona (1895–1963), a Cuban who studied briefly under Maurice Ravel in Paris, composed operas in the 1930s in Havana and movie music in Hollywood in the forties, before reverting back to his old loves of rumba and danza. Tania Kross combined this music with the voodoo songs of Heitor Villa-Lobos and a traditional Curaçaoan tambú, arranged by Randal Corsen, called *Nonze su kantika di tambú*. This is without a doubt the most beautiful tambú ever sung, but what is even more remarkable is that Kross and Corsen opted for a string quartet to accompany it, something one would not expect at all from a lament from the days of slavery.

Accents have indeed shifted: classical performances are going more toward Latin jazz, from the African tambour accompaniment to that of that cello and viola that weep the rhythm. Anything goes in the twenty-first century; everything is mixed and blended. But classical Antillean music is not dead by a long shot.

Of course older Curaçaoans shake their heads when they hear the new interpretations of the old masters. Elderly Argentines wanted nothing to do with Astor Piazzolla, who introduced both classical music (he took piano lessons from Nadia Boulanger in Paris) and jazz (he grew up in the United States) to the tango. Without Piazzolla, tango would have withered away on the vine. He modernized it.

For his jazz CD *Evolushon*, Randal Corsen used the Antillean waltz, danza, and tambú. For the tambú he called in the help of American tenor saxophonist David Sánchez. Together they explored the furthest boundaries of polyrhythmic playing. The tambú may have originally been the Dutch Antillean blues, but it can sound like free jazz when the rhythm is cut loose. In Corsen's view, you do not make jazz out of salsa, rumba, or tambú simply by sticking in long solos. Jazz is a language; the essence of jazz is that it allows the musician to break open the music, to create space for himself. The pianist reacts to the bassist and the drummer and vice versa; a conversation takes place. And that conversation can take place just as easily on the basis of a waltz, danza, mazurka, or tambú as it can on that of bebop or swing. With one consequence: you can no longer dance to jazz.

That which characterizes Antillean music the most gets lost in the end.

34

The Trade Wind in My Ears

I left Curaçao in 2002. Back in Amsterdam I was able almost immediately to organize an Antillean music evening. The offer came from De Ijsbreker (The Icebreaker), the Center for Contemporary Music in Amsterdam, which invites an author every year to program a concert. At De Ijsbreker's expense I was able to let Johnny Kleinmoedig come to the Netherlands. I was also allowed to commission a work. I agonized for quite a while whether it ought to be from Robert Rojer or Wim Statius Muller, and in the end I opted for the latter. He composed the three-part work *Suite Pikiña*, which was performed by the Calefax Woodwind Quartet. It consisted of a waltz, a mazurka, and a tumba.

A day before the concert I was a guest on the Dutch radio program A4, on the Radio 4 classical music broadcast. The journalist interviewing me, Lex Bohlmeijer, asked me if the howling trade winds that blew on Curaçao had affected my hearing. Judging from the interviews I had published at the outset of my career in the Dutch weekly magazine *Haagse Post*, I had to know how to separate the wheat from the chaff when it came to music; I had gone along on tour with such renowned musicians as Youri Egorov, Bernhard Haitink, Elly Ameling, Vera Beths, Anner Bijlsma, Emmy Verhey, Ivo Pogorelic, and Katia and Marielle Labeque. How could I make such a plea for those trivial little Antillean waltzes?

A little prodding is not a bad thing to liven up a conversation, but scorn is the other extreme. I felt my blood starting to boil. For three centuries the European powers had ruled the Caribbean islands, for three centuries they thought only their culture was of any value. Step by step, Antilleans tried to emancipate themselves. They made Antillean waltzes and mazurkas out of European ones. And what does the Radio 4 journalist accuse them of? "Dubious forms of imitation."

I cannot recall exactly what my reply was. In any case, I know I made an argument for music I had never, ever heard in the Netherlands. To end the program, there was a horribly performed piece of music composed by Wim Statius Muller to prove that Dutch Antillean music was worthless. I left the studio feeling like I had just attended a session of the Colonial Council.

The painful thing is that the Dutch radically change their opinion when it comes to South American composers. They bow deeply to a pianist such as the Brazilian Nelson Freire. In Amsterdam he performed the piece *Bachianas Brasileiras* by his countryman Heitor Villa-Lobos. Analogous to Caribbean composers, Villa-Lobos (1887–1959) had followed the example of European composers, of Bach. And what did the reviewer in Amsterdam's De Volkskrant write? "Glissandi as light as a feather, rhythmically sharp as a knife. Villa-Lobos's masterpiece radiated such *joie de vivre* as though Johann Sebastian Bach were celebrating carnival in Rio."

Isn't this a case of applying double standards?

I left the studio to attend the dress rehearsal. The members of Calefax Woodwind Quartet would be going through their final run of *Suite Pikiña,* and for the first time in the presence of the composer. How would they react to his music? With as much disdain as the radio journalist?

The Calefax woodwind players had a problem. The rhythm of the tumba was so ingenious they were wondering how they ought to interpret the various jumps. Oh yes, they had played Duke Ellington, but that was child's play compared to the tumba. They asked Statius Muller to tap along with the rhythm. It did not help at first. To clarify matters, he made drawings of the rhythmic patterns on a piece of paper. I saw the eagerness on the musician's faces as if they had discovered some new dimension in rhythmics. They tried again, taking it from the top. And again everything fell apart in the final measures of the tumba. Wim jumped up on stage. "Look here," he said with his Antillean accent. "The dancers had to take small steps." He whirled around the piano to the oboe player. "The dance venues were small. And the women had those big, big behinds." That did the trick, and the musicians finally got the hang of it.

That evening, on March 27, 2003, De Rode Hoed Theater in Amsterdam was packed to the rafters. The audience of four hundred and fifty gave Johnny Kleinmoedig, Wim Statius Muller, and the Calefax Quartet a standing ovation. It came as a surprise to the Antillean musicians; they had gone on stage as though they were taking an exam and, in their own estimation, they had not done so well. It proved to be much better than that, even though they were visibly tense at the start of the concert, realizing they had to overcome prejudice note by note. They had wanted to do that with more conviction, as they had done during the encore, a four-handed improvisation on an old waltz that Wim Statius Muller had learned from his father. Only then did they feel a wave of warmth sweep through the theater, and only then was it possible for them to shed every shred of anxiety.

After the concert, and a few drinks with the musicians, while walking home along the canals, I remembered my last *atardi* on Curaçao. My bags were packed; most of my belongings had been shipped. I was sitting on the porch looking out over green ocean, watching the dolphins leaping out of the water for the last time, the frigate birds and pelicans diving for fish, the flamingoes returning to their salt pans, the sun setting behind the ships moored at the docks waiting for permission to enter the harbor. I heard the final warbling trills of the trupial songbirds, smelled one last time the cloying sweet scent of the *barba di yonkuman*, cooling myself with a fan for one last time. And far in the distance I could hear a waltz being played in a house on a piano that was out of tune.

I bid farewell to an island, to an era. I said goodbye to a certain way of living, to warmth and exuberance. And I said farewell to the waltzes, mazurkas, and tumbas.

Without that music I would have left the Dutch Antilles with less wistfulness; without that music I would have led a much barer existence, it would have been much harsher, like the volcanic stone on which you cannot walk in your bare feet. Yes, I was white, and nowhere did I feel as white as I did living in the Netherlands Antilles. But the music took away the sharp edges.

35

The Bastard Son

Something else happened during that concert. A young man approached me during intermission. He was short, a little on the chubby side, balding, with a slightly dark complexion and a pair of dark eyes glowing with a friendly look behind a pair of old-fashioned glasses. I shook his hand saying, "Hello Edgar." As soon as the name escaped my lips, I realized I had make a terrible mistake; Edgar Palm had been dead for years.

"My father," said the man with a pride that quickly faded when his voice started to quiver.

"My very own father. But I only just found out. Since my mother died, to be precise. Just before she died, she told me who my father was."

Edgar had lived with her in her house when he had come to study in Holland at the Intermediate Polytechnic School. And Palms will be Palms—crazy about women. Edgar had had an affair with his landlady, who was considerably older than he was, and she had gotten pregnant soon afterward.

The son had always been surprised he had such dark skin, much browner than that of his brothers and sisters. Not really more than that. He had never asked about it; his mother was as Dutch as raw herring with onions, and his father, too. Sixty years later he would hear his father had been his stepfather and that Edgar Palm had actually been his biological father.

When his mother died he traveled to Curaçao. He went to visit Edgar's legitimate children, introducing himself as their half brother, something they did not really appreciate. He could not talk to Edgar himself, since he had passed away a few months earlier.

On the island he learned who Edgar had been: a musician and a composer, descendant of a famous musical family. He bought a CD of his father's recordings, bought a stack of music scores, and copied others at the Central Archives. Back in Holland, he immersed himself in a study of his father's music, to the best of his ability. It had been a long time since he had been able to read music, and he had forgotten about the ins and outs of sharps and flats.

That evening in Theater De Rode Hoed was just what the doctor ordered. He could finally hear his father's music being performed by musicians from Curaçao. He had taken a small tape recorder with him to secretly record the concert. The music would tell more about who his father was than any photograph or letter.

"It was like a whole book opening up in front of me," he told me. "A history book about my father and my descendants. I suddenly belong to another world and other people, to Swedes who turned into Dutch Antilleans on the other side of the Atlantic, to composers who built a bridge between Europe and Afro-Caribbean music, to pianists, clarinetists, organists who played in the synagogue in the morning, in the lodge, and evenings and nights at garden parties, in a club or a bar . . ."

He would go on to further examine the whole history, down to the smallest details. He would go back to Curaçao to gather more information. And then he would make one last journey. No, he would not put flowers in a vase on his father's grave; he would honor him in another way. Just the way Edgar would have wanted, he would go to Warsaw. He would lay a wreath of flowers before Chopin's heart.

GLOSSARY

tambú—the name of a drum, dance, and rhythm descended from Africa and danced, sung, and played by descendants of slaves.

December murders—in 1982, fifteen opponents to the military regime of Desi Bouterse were murdered in Paramaribo—they included journalists, union officials, politicians, members of the intelligentsia (e.g., doctors and lawyers). At this writing a trial against Bouterse and several others accused of their murder has resumed in Paramaribo.

mondi—Papiamentu word for bush, uncultivated land.

Karl Friedrich May (February 25, 1842–March 30, 1912) was a popular German writer, noted mainly for adventure novels set in the American Old West (best known for the characters of *Winnetou* and *Old Shatterhand*); not well known in the United States.

Ossip Zadkine (Russian: July 14, 1890–November 25, 1967) was a Belarusian-born artist who lived in France. He is primarily known as a sculptor, but also produced paintings and lithographs.

makamba—word in Papiamentu to denote a white person of Dutch origin.

SOURCES AND BIBLIOGRAPHY

Bastet, Frederic. *Helse Liefde, over Marie d' Aguoult, Frédéric Chopin, Franz Liszt, George Sand*. Amsterdam, 1997.

Bellamy, Olivier. *Le pays don't le Prince est un piano*, Le Monde de la Musique. Paris, September 2004.

Berlioz, Hector. *Mijn leven, twee delen* (My Life, two volumes). Amsterdam, 1987.

Berry-Haseth, Lucille, Broek, Aart G., Joubert, Sidney M. *Pa Saka Kara, Antologia di literature Papiamentu, tomo 1*. Willemstad, Curaçao, 1998.

Broek, Aart G. *Pa saka kara; Historia di literatura papiamentu*. Willemstad, Curaçao, 1998.

Broek, Aart G. *Chris J. H. Engels: proeve van een dossier*. Willemstad, Curaçao, 1997.

Buddingh', Bernard R. *Van Punt en Snoa, Onstaan en groei van Willemstad, Curaçao vanaf 1634* (From the Point and Snoa, Founding and growth of Willemstad, Curaçao since 1634). 's-Hertogenbosch, 1994.

Burger, Ernst. *Fréderic Chopin, Eine Lebenschroniek in Bilderen und Dokumenten*. München, 1990.

Carpentier, Alejo. *La Música en Cuba*. Havana, 1988.

Corsen, Joseph S. *Senjor Redactor, ingezonden brief in La Cruz van 6 December 1905* (Mr. Editor, letter to the editor in the December 6, 1905 issue of *La Cruz*). Manuscript in the library of the Universidad Nashonal di Antia, Willemstad, Curaçao.

Debrot, Cola. *Verzameld werk I: Over Antilliaanse cultuur verzorgd door Jules de Pakm* (Collected Work vol. I: On Dutch Antillean Culture, edited by Pierre H. Dubois). Amsterdam, 1985.

———. *Verzameld werk III: Verhalen, verzorgd door Pierre H. Dubois* (Collected Work vol. III: Stories, edited by Pierre H. Dubois). Amsterdam, 1986.

Eisler, Benita. *Requiem voor Chopin*. Amsterdam, 2003.

Emmanuel, I. S. and S. A. *History of the Jews of the Netherlands Antilles*. Cincinnati, 1970.

Engels, Chris J., and Van der Walle, J. *Klein Venetië, Curaçao in vroeger dagen* (Little Venice, Curaçao in Earlier Days). 's-Hertogenbosch, 1990.

García Márquez, Gabriel. *Leven om het te vertellen* (Living to Tell the Tale). Amsterdam, 2003.

Gottschalk, Louis Moreau. *Notes of a Pianist*. New York, 1964.

Habibe, Henry. *Un herida bida ta; Een verkenning van het poëtisch oeuvre van Pierre Lauffer* (A Wounded Life: An investigation into the poetic oeuvre of Pierre Lauffer). Willemstad, Curaçao, 1994.

———. "Waarom ATARDI niet zo maar een gedicht is" (Why ATARDI is not just a poem). *Beurs-en Nieuwsberichten*. Willemstad, Curaçao, June 16, 1990.

Halman, J. J. M. *Op weg naar San Hilarión: impressies van enkele reisgenoten* (On the Road to San Hilarión: Impressions by a few travelling companions). Willemstad, Curaçao, 2004.

Hamel, Réginald. *Louis Moreau Gottschalk et son temps*. Montréal, 1996.

Hartog, Joh. *Geschiedenis van de Nederlandse Antillen* in twee delen (History of the Netherlands Antilles in two volumes). Oranjestad, Aruba 1961.

———. *Journalistiek leven in Curaçao* (Journalistic Life in Curaçao). Willemstad, Curaçao, 1944.

———. *Het verhaal der Maduro's* (The Story of the Maduro Family). Oranjestad, Aruba, 1962.

Hoetink, H. *Het patroon van de Oude Curaçaose Samenleving: een sociologische studie* (The Patron in Old Curaçao Society: A sociological study). Assen, 1958.

Horst, Lisbeth van der. *Wereldoorlog in de West: Suriname de Nederlandse Antillen en Aruba 1940–1945* (World War in the Dutch West Indies: Surinam, the Netherlands Antilles and Aruba 1940–1945). Amsterdam, 2004.

Huijers, Dolf, and Ezechiëls, Lucky. *Landhuizen van Curaçao en Bonaire* (Country Estates of Curaçao and Bonaire). Amsterdam, 1992.

Juliana, Elis. "De tamboe op Curaçao" (The Tambú on Curaçao). *Bzzlletin* 16, The Hague, 1987.

Krafft, A. J. C. *Historie en oude families van de Nederlandse Antillen* (History and Old Families of the Netherlands Antilles). The Hague, 1951.

Lampe, H. E. *Aruba voorheen en thans* (Aruba Then and Now). The Hague, 1932.

Leeuwen, Boeli van. "Patriarch met trio, Ode aan de Curaçaose Familie Palm." *Beurs-en Nieuwsberichten*. Willemstad, March 14, 1987.

Liszt, Franz. *Chopin*. Paris, 1851.

Maduro, J. M. L. "De Portuguese Joden in Curaçao." *Gedenkboek* 14, March 1987.

Man, Herman de. "Het zingende eiland." *Neerlandia* (Dutch Antillean edition), October 1944.

Meeteren, Nicolaas van. *Volkskunde van Curaçao* (Folklore of Curaçao). Willemstad, Curaçao, 1947.

Meunier, Jean-Pierre. "De Saint-Pierre à Paris." Liner note text to CD *Biguine, Valse et Mazurka créoles*. Paris, 1993.

Morón, Norman. "Homenahe na Otrobanda" (Homage to Otrobanda). Liner note text to CD of the same name. Willemstad, Curaçao, 2000.

Oversteegen, J. J. *In het schuim van grauwe wolken, Het leven van Cola Debrot tot 1948* (In the Spume of Grey Clouds: The Life of Cola Debrot to 1948). Amsterdam, 1994.

———. *Gemunt op wederkeer, Het leven van Cola Debrot vanaf 1948* (Intent on Returning: The Life of Cola Debrot from 1948). Amsterdam, 1994.

Ozinga, M. D. *De monumenten van Curaçao in woord en beeld* (Monuments of Curaçao in words and illustrations). Willemstad, Curaçao, 1959.

Palm, Edgar. *Muziek en musici van de Nederlandse Antillen* (Music and Musicians of the Netherlands Antilles). Willemstad, Curaçao, 1978.

Palm, Jules de. *Julio Perrenal: Dichters van het Papiaments Lied* (Julio Perrenal: Poet of Papiamento Song). Amsterdam, 1979.

Pool, John de. *Bolivar en Curaçao, Leyenda histórica* (Bolivar and Curaçao, Historical legend). Zutphen, 1988.

———. *Del Curaçao que se va.* Panama, 1935.

Prunetti Winkel, Pauline, *Scharloo: A nineteenth century quarter of Willemstad, Curaçao.* Curaçao, 1990.

Quevedo, Raymond. *Kaiso: A short history of Trinidad Calypso.* St. Augustine, 1983.

Reinders, Alex. *Politieke geschiedenis van de Nederlandse Antillen en Aruba 1950–1993* (Political History of the Netherlands Antilles and Aruba 1950–1993). Zutphen, 1993.

Rohler, Gordon. *Calypso and Society in Pre-independence Trinidad.* Port of Spain, 1990.

Rojer, Robert A. "Een muzikale wandering van Chopin naar de Curaçaose dansa" (A musical stroll from Chopin to the Curaçaoan danza). *U.N.A. Cahier* 32. Willemstad, Curaçao, 1990 (University of the Netherlands Antilles).

———. *Vanuit de blauwzwarte diepte, Marcus Dahlhaus en Martinus Niewindt; een cultuurhistorisch essay* (From the Blue Black Deeps: Marcus Dahlhaus and Martinus Niewindt; a cultural historical essay). Rotterdam, 1997.

Römer, Robert A., *Een volk op weg. Un pueblo na kaminda: een sociologisch historisch studie van de Curaçaose samenleving* (A People on Its Way: A socio-historical study of Curaçaoan society). Zutphen, 1979.

———. *Otrobanda, het verhaal van een stadswijk* (Otrobanda, the story of a city quarter). Willemstad, Curaçao, 1994.

Rooy, René A. de. "De miskennig van Julio Perrenal" (The Failure to Appreciate Julio Perrenal). *Eldorado* 1-12. Willemstad, Curaçao, 1949.

Ros, Martin. *Vuurnacht, Toussaint Louverture en de slavenopstand op Haïti* (Night of Fire: Toussaint Louverture and the slave revolt on Haiti). Amsterdam, 1991.

Rosalia, René V. *Tambú, de legale en kerkelijke repressie van Afro-Curaçaose volksuitingen* (Tambú, the legal and clerical repression of expressions of Afro-Curaçaoan folk culture). Zutphen, 1997.

Rubinstein, Arthur. *My Young Years.* New York, 1976.

———. *My Many Years.* New York, 1980.

Rutten, A. M. G. *Leven en muziekwerken van de dichter-musicus J. S. Corsen* (Life and Musical Works of the Poet Musician J. S. Corsen). Assen, 1983.

Starr, S. Frederick. *Bamboula: The Life and Times of Louis Moreau Gottschalk.* New York, 1995.

Statius Muller, W. "Enkele aantekeningen over de Antilliaanse dansmuziek" (A Few Notes on Dutch Antillean dance music). *Christoffel*. Willemstad, Curaçao, June 1956.

Teenstra, M. D. *De Nederlandsche West-Indische eilanden* (The Dutch West Indian Islands). Amsterdam, 1836.

Vey Mestdagh, Karel de. *Onder een hemel van tin* (Under a Sky of Tin). The Hague, 2005.

Visman, M. A. *Mijn jeugd op Curaçao* (My Childhood on Curaçao). Leersum, 1993.

Wolf, Tim de. *Discography of Music from the Netherlands Antilles & Aruba*. Zutphen, 1999.

———. "The record labels Hoyco and Musika." From liners notes to the CD *Riba Dempel, Otrabanda Records*. Amsterdam, 2003.

Zielinski, Tadeusz A. *Fréderic Chopin*. Paris, 1995.

Zoon, Cees. "Over Tip Marugg." Interview in Dutch newspaper *De Volkskrant*. May 20, 1988.

Much valuable information was gathered through conversations and interviews with the following people: Gilbert (Gibi) Bacilio, Mighty Bomber, Eric den Brabander, Aart G. Broek, Hortence Brouwn, Bernard Buddingh', Izaline Calister, Ephraim Cijntje, Randal Corsen, Frank Davelaar, Nydia Ecury, Henry Habibe, Carel de Haseth, Chila de Haseth-Bolivar, May Henriquez-Alvares Correa, Max Henriquez, Diane Henriquez, Nicole Henriquez, Livio Hermans, Elmer Joubert, Johnny Kleinmoedig, Boeli van Leeuwen, Frank Martinus Arion, Tip Marugg, Marjo Nederlof, Edgar Palm, Frieda Palm-Palm, Walter Palm, Robert Rojer, René A. Römer, Jacqueline Römer, Marijke Schweitz, Millicent (Dudi) Smeets-Muskus, Wim Statius Muller, Sally Statius Muller-Führing.

Special thanks are in order to: Aart G. Broek, Emile Brugman, Izaline Calister, Randal Corsen, Marre van Dantzig, Livio Hermans, Robert Rojer, Millicent (Dudi) Smeets-Muskus, Wim Statius Muller, and Alban Wesley, who read the manuscript and provided me with commentary and feedback. Naturally I take sole responsibility as to the accuracy of the facts and their interpretation.

I am greatly indebted to Hendrik Beers. With the help of Carel de Haseth, he sorted out all the details of the Palm family tree. Beers put all the data online, which I could consult while writing the text.

DISCOGRAPHY

Harold Martina. *Danza!* (twenty-five Caribbean dances, with works by Louis Moreau Gottschalk, Jules Blasini, Joseph Sickman Corsen, Robert Rojer). S. E. L. Maduro Muziekstichting, 1992.

Edgar Palm and Charles Sweers. *Dulce Scharloo* (twelve dances and waltzes by Jacobo Conrad). S. E. L. Maduro Muziekstichting, 1993.

Wim Statius Muller *Antillean Dances, Opus 4* (twenty-five waltzes, and tumbas). S. E. L. Maduro Muziekstichting & René Gailly International Productions, 1990.

———. *Antillean Dances, Opus 2,4,5,6* (fifty-six waltzes, mazurkas, and tumbas, danzas, calypsos). Qualunque, 2005.

Livio Hermans. *Edgar Palm* (seventeen waltzes, mazurkas, tumbas). René Gailly International Productions, Ghent, Belgium, 1994.

Robert Rojer and Harold Martina. *Robert Rojer* (twelve Curaçaoan waltzes for two pianos). René Gailly International Productions, Ghent, Belgium, 1988.

Joseph Sickman Corsen. *Curaçao Waltzes of the 19th Century*. Selwyn J. Maduro, 2000.

Riba Dempel: Popular Dance Music of Curaçao 1950-1954. Otrabanda Records & Music, Amsterdam, 2003.

Harold Martina. *J. M. Emirto de Lima*. S.E.L. Maduro Muziekstichting, 2005.

Norman Morón. *Homenahe na Otrobanda* (waltzes, dances, and mazurkas by Charles Maduro, Alfonso Da Costa Gomez, Philip E. Quast, Jacobo Palm, J. O. Boskaljon, Albert Palm, Jules Blasini, and Norman Morón). FdcG, 2001.

Padú del Caribe. *Collection no. 1*. Selwyn J. Maduro, CCF, 2005.

Oswin "Chin" Behilia. *Bendishon disfrasá*. Otrabanda Records & Music, Amsterdam, 2002.

———. *Live*. Otrabanda Records & Music, Amsterdam, 2006.

Liber. Otrabanda Records & Music, Amsterdam, 2009.

Erwin Prudencia. *Transishon*. Erwin Prudencia Productions, 2000.

Izaline Calister. *Soño di un muhé*. Exil Muzik, 2001.

———. *Mariposa*. Eazy C Productions, 2002.

———. *Krioyo*. Network Medien, 2004.

———. *Kanta Hélele*. Network Medien, 2006.

———. *Speranza*. Brigadoon/Flow Records, 2009.

———. *Kandela*. Eazy C Productions, 2012.

Philip Martin. *Piano Music by Louis Moreau Gottschalk* (seven CDs). Hyperion Records, London, 1990–2004.

Georges Rabol. *Gottschalk, Cervantes, Saumell.* Opus 111, Paris, 1993.

Alan Marks and Nerine Barrett. *Gottschalk, Piano Music for 2 and 4 hands.* Nimbus, 2000.

Randal Corsen. *Evolushon.* A-Records, 2003.

Randal Corsen. *Armonia.* AJA Records, 2007.

Randal Corsen and Friends. *Dulsura di Korsou: Contemporary Music from Curaçao.* AJA Records, 2008.

Randal Corsen. *Corsen Plays Corsen* (twenty-three works by Joseph Sickman Corsen). S. E. L. Maduro Muziekstichting, Willemstad, 2005.

Alexandre Stellio, l' Orchestre Antillais, et al. *Biguine, Valse et Mazurka Créoles.* Frémeaux & Associés, Paris, 1993.

Tania Kross. *Corazón.* Universal-Philips, 2005.

Grupo Zamanakitoki. *Kaya Grandi.* PAN Records, 1996 (all compositions by its leader Eric Calmes).

INDEX

CPSIA information can be obtained at www.ICGtesting.com
Printed in the USA
BVOW05*0620151214

378303BV00001B/1/P

9 781628 461855